BROTHER'S KEEPER

by Mahad Ali

❙❙SAMUEL FRENCH❙❙

Copyright © 2023 by Mahad Ali
Cover design by Martha Hegarty
All Rights Reserved

MY BROTHER'S KEEPER is fully protected under the copyright laws of the British Commonwealth, including Canada, the United States of America, and all other countries of the Copyright Union. All rights, including professional and amateur stage productions, recitation, lecturing, public reading, motion picture, radio broadcasting, television, online/digital production, and the rights of translation into foreign languages are strictly reserved.

ISBN 978-0-573-13380-0

concordtheatricals.co.uk
concordtheatricals.com

FOR AMATEUR PRODUCTION ENQUIRIES

UNITED KINGDOM AND WORLD
EXCLUDING NORTH AMERICA
licensing@concordtheatricals.co.uk
020-7054-7298

Each title is subject to availability from Concord Theatricals, depending upon country of performance.

CAUTION: Professional and amateur producers are hereby warned that *MY BROTHER'S KEEPER* is subject to a licensing fee. The purchase, renting, lending or use of this book does not constitute a licence to perform this title(s), which licence must be obtained from the appropriate agent prior to any performance. Performance of this title(s) without a licence is a violation of copyright law and may subject the producer and/or presenter of such performances to penalties. Both amateurs and professionals considering a production are strongly advised to apply to the appropriate agent before starting rehearsals, advertising, or booking a theatre. A licensing fee must be paid whether the title is presented for charity or gain and whether or not admission is charged.

This work is published by Samuel French, an imprint of Concord Theatricals Ltd.

The Professional Rights in this play are controlled The Agency (London) Ltd., 24 Pottery Lane, Holland Park, London, W11 4LZ.

No one shall make any changes in this title for the purpose of production. No part of this book may be reproduced, stored in a retrieval system, scanned, uploaded, or transmitted in any form, by any means, now known or yet to be invented, including mechanical, electronic, digital, photocopying, recording, videotaping, or otherwise, without the prior written permission of the publisher. No one shall share this title, or part of this title, to any social media or file hosting websites.

The moral right of Mahad Ali to be identified as author of this work has been asserted in accordance with Section 77 of the Copyright, Designs and Patents Act 1988.

USE OF COPYRIGHTED MUSIC

A licence issued by Concord Theatricals to perform this play does not include permission to use the incidental music specified in this publication. In the United Kingdom: Where the place of performance is already licensed by the PERFORMING RIGHT SOCIETY (PRS) a return of the music used must be made to them. If the place of performance is not so licensed then application should be made to PRS for Music (www.prsformusic.com). A separate and additional licence from PHONOGRAPHIC PERFORMANCE LTD (www.ppluk.com) may be needed whenever commercial recordings are used. Outside the United Kingdom: Please contact the appropriate music licensing authority in your territory for the rights to any incidental music.

USE OF COPYRIGHTED THIRD-PARTY MATERIALS

Licensees are solely responsible for obtaining formal written permission from copyright owners to use copyrighted third-party materials (e.g., artworks, logos) in the performance of this play and are strongly cautioned to do so. If no such permission is obtained by the licensee, then the licensee must use only original materials that the licensee owns and controls. Licensees are solely responsible and liable for clearances of all third-party copyrighted materials, and shall indemnify the copyright owners of the play(s) and their licensing agent, Concord Theatricals Ltd., against any costs, expenses, losses and liabilities arising from the use of such copyrighted third-party materials by licensees.

IMPORTANT BILLING AND CREDIT REQUIREMENTS

If you have obtained performance rights to this title, please refer to your licensing agreement for important billing and credit requirements.

MY BROTHER'S KEEPER was first produced by Relentless Productions on 14th February 2023 at Theatre503. The cast was as follows:

AMAN . . . . Tapiwa Mugweni

HASSAN . . . . Tito Williams

AIDAN BRADLEY . . . . .Oscar Adams

BILL BRADLEY . . . . .Phillip Wright

LINTON HUGHES . . . . Peter Eastland

Writer and Co-Producer – **Mahad Ali**

Director – **Robert Awosusi**

Co-Producer – **Layla Madanat** (**She/Her**)

Designer – **Amanda Ramasawmy** (**She/Her**)

Production Manager – **Emily Dickson** (**She/Her**)

Stage Manager – **Aiman Bandali** (**She/Her**)

Placement Assistant Stage Manager – **Emily Compton** (**She/Her**)

Lighting Designer – **Kieron Johnson** (**They/Them**)

Sound Designer – **Esther Kehinde Ajayi** (**She/Her/They**)

Poster Design – **Martha Hegarty**

CAST

OSCAR ADAMS
Oscar Adams is an actor from Bristol, recently
graduated from the Oxford School of Drama. This is
his professional London stage debut.

PETER EASTLAND
Peter Eastland trained at the Webber Douglas
Academy of Dramatic Art.
Theatre credits include: *Othello, All of Us, Mourning
Becomes Electra, Three Sisters, The Relapse, The
Winter's Tale* and *The Cherry Orchard* (Royal National
Theatre); *Only The Lonely* (Birmingham Rep);
Northanger Abbey (Theatre Royal, Northampton); *Dangerous Liaisons,
Over A Barrel* and *Romeo and Juliet* (Everyman, Cheltenham); *The
Wedding* (Young Vic); *Anna Weiss* (Cockpit); *The Love Child* (Red
Shift); *Hamlet* and *Rozencrantz and Guildenstern Are Dead* (Moving
Theatre); *The Stories We Tell Each Other (And The Stories We Tell
Ourselves)* (Taunton Brewhouse); *Afterwards* and *Better* (Spare Parts);
Black Atlas (London Shakespeare Workout) and *Life's A Dream* (Players
& Co).
TV credits include: *The Basil Brush Show, Waking The Dead, Casualty,
Small Potatoes, Telequest, The Fractured Man, Galois' Enduring Legacy*
and *Inside The Wolf's Lair*.
Short film includes: *Going Postal*.

PHILIP WRIGHT
Theatre credits include: *Hot Lane, Dirty Laundry,
Ugly Duck* (Claybody Theatre); *The House They Grew
Up In* (Chichester Festival Theatre); *Jumpy* (Theatr
Clwyd); *Tutto Bene Mama* (The Print Room); *The
Knotty, The Tempest, Macbeth, The Norman Conquests,
Dangerous Corner, The Plough & The Stars, Eric The
Epic* (New Vic Theatre, Stoke); *As You Like It* (Bristol
Old Vic/West Yorkshire Playhouse); *The Baby* (The Bush); *The Best
Man* (Croydon Warehouse); *Twelfth Night, The Threepenny Opera; The
Gambler* (London Bubble); *Macbeth, As Is* (Half Moon); *Privates on
Parade, Death of a Salesman* (Birmingham Rep); *Made in Bangkok, As
You Like It* (Belgrade Theatre, Coventry); *Everyman* (Upstream); *Dick
Whittington* (Milford Haven).

TV credits include: *Cobra, The 6th Commandment, Endeavour, The Baby, EastEnders, Save Me Too, Casualty, The Rook, Call The Midwife, Good Omens, The Innocents, Doctor Foster, Berlin Station, Silent Witness, Line of Duty, A Mother's Son, Fast Freddie, Waking the Dead, Enid, Law and Order, The Fixer, Never Better, The Infinite World of HG Wells, Ultimate Force, Poirot, William & Mary, Living It, Messiah, At Home With The Braithwaites, Paparazzo, The Vice, Dangerous Lady, Maid Marian & Her Merry Men, Prime Suspect (1, 2 and 3).*
Film credits include: *Rogue Agent; Mad, Bad and Sad; The Flying Scotsman; Saving Grace.*

TAPIWA MUGWENI
Theatre credits include: *The Polar Express* (Site Specific); *A Midsummer Night's Dream* (Virginia Tech University); *The Laramie Project* (Virginia Tech University); *Joe Turner's Come and Gone* (Young Vic).
TV credits include: *Chewing Gum* (Retort and Channel 4); *The Innocents* (Netflix).
Film credits include: *Stan & Ollie* (BBC Films).

TITO WILLIAMS
Tito Williams trained at East 15 and Drama St Mary's.
TV credits include: *Zen School of Motoring* (BBC).

CREATIVE TEAM

WRITER – MAHAD ALI (HE/HIM)

My Brother's Keeper is part of the 22/23 season at Theatre503 after being selected as part of their 503Five programme. He has recently been selected to be a part of the 2022/23 Sky Comedy Rep with Birmingham Rep and Sky Studios. Mahad was a part of the inaugural Tamasha Theatre Playwriting group and has had performances at Stratford Theatre Royal Stratford East, Rich Mix, Park and Soho Theatre with Tamasha and Paines Plough. Mahad was part of BBC Studios Writers Academy 2021, where he worked on continuing drama series. He is developing TV comedy/drama ideas which share the fun, joy and pain of the Black British African experience.

DIRECTOR – ROB AWOSUSI (HE/HIM)

Robert is a director/writer/dramaturg/theatremaker currently based in London, making art about people not listened to. He creates performance work (live and recorded) that explores socio-political issues, championing and uplifting marginalised voices and communities in meaningful and stimulating worlds; current personal focuses are around Blackness, capitalism and climate change.

Work includes: *hang (LAMDA), JASMINE. HOME. MOTHER* (Young Vic); *Bullring Techno Makeout Jamz* (The Bunker); *Our Tower* (The Arcola); *The Derek Smith Show* (Mountview); *phroot sahlad* (Tour); *The Lost* (Young Vic).

As Associate director: *Radio Elusia Podcast* (Boundless), *WE KNOW NOT WHAT WE MAY BE* [Artistic Associate] (Barbican).

As Assistant director: *Constellations* (Donmar/Vaudeville); *"Daddy" – A Melodrama* (Almeida); *Fairview* (Young Vic); *Let Kilburn Shake* (Kiln); *The Trial* (Young Vic).

Other work includes: *Made at Home: A Virtual Scratch* (Tamasha), *Coronaville Delivery Service.*

Robert has previous been Resident Director for the Almeida Theatre and a part of the RE: Assemble programme with Paines Plough. He served on the Advisory Board for Boundless Theatre, and on the Board Shadowing Programme run by Artistic Directors of the Future.

PRODUCER – LAYLA MADANAT (SHE/HER)

Layla is a freelance creative producer, artist and activist. She combines creative and socially engaged approaches to create live relationships between arts projects and social justice causes. After graduating with a Master's in Gender, Development, and Globalisation from LSE, she worked in classical music before transitioning into a freelance career across the Arts and Social Impact Sector.

As a Producer she is currently part of the Stage One Bridge the Gap cohort. As a Director, she was most recently Assistant Director to Pooja

Ghai on Hakawatis at the Sam Wanamaker Playhouse at Shakespeare's Globe. Her short documentary *mosaic/فسيفساء*, co-created with Eleanor Nawal, was selected for the BFI London Film Festival Works-in-Progress Showcase 2021, and Sheffield Doc Fest 2021.
She has worked in the UK with organisations such as the Rose Theatre, Shubbak Festival, Theatre Deli, and across Europe with The Walk Productions, walking Europe with Little Amal as Assistant Producer and Associate to the Artistic Director. She is a freelance research and analysis lead for social justice organisations Sikh Forgiveness and Spark and Co. Layla is the Co-Producer for Relentless Productions, Co-Founded with Mahad Ali in 2022.

DESIGNER – AMANDA RAMASAWMY (SHE/HER)
Amanda is a visual artist from London who works across performance design, production design and video.
Recent theatre work includes: *The Seven Pomegranate Seeds* (Rose Theatre, UK) Associate Designer; *Mephisto: A Rhapsody* (Gate Theatre, UK) Assistant Designer. As an artist she has created work for Barbican Centre, Art Night, Flat Time House, Central School of Speech and Drama and Toronto Arts Media Centre.

PRODUCTION MANAGER – EMILY DICKSON (SHE/HER)
Emily studied a M.A in Collaborative Theatre Production and Design at Guildhall School of Music and Drama. She is a founding member of the production company Lost Tapir Productions.
Her most recent credits include: Production Manager for *CashMoney Now* (The Big House); Stage Manager for *1797: The Mariner's Revenge* (HistoryRiot) and Stage and Production Manager for *run, Rabbit, run* (Levantes Dance Theatre).

STAGE MANAGER – AIMAN BANDALI (SHE/HER)
Aiman trained at LAMDA on their Production and Technical Arts course where her main focus was Stage and Production management. She went on to do the optional BA year where she specialised in company management and achieved a First Class Honours Degree. Some of her roles include: ASM on *Hakawatis: The Women of the Arabian Nights* at The Sam Wanamaker Playhouse; Production Manager for *Don Carlos, New England, Love Steals Us From Loneliness.* She also was CSM for *Little Shop of Horrors* Musical and *Earthquakes in London.*

PLACEMENT ASSISTANT STAGE MANAGER – EMILY COMPTON (SHE/HER)
Emily is 2022 FdA Production & Technical Arts: Stage & Screen Specialism Production & Stage Management student at LAMDA.

LIGHTING DESIGNER – KIERON JOHNSON (THEY/THEM)

Lighting Designer for Theatre, Opera, Dance and Live Performance Art Professional Member of the Association for Lighting Production and Design ALPD Lumierè 20:20.

SOUND DESIGNER – ESTHER KEHINDE AJAYI (SHE/HER/THEY)

Esther Kehinde Ajayi is a West London based Sound Artist. Esther enjoys exploring the nuances of the human condition through the use of tone, texture, SFX and melody. Esther is currently studying Sound Arts at the University of Arts London and excited to begin incorporating technology, performance and installation into her practice. Esther is currently an associate artist at the London theatre company Tiata Fahodzi. Sound Design Credits include: *Cash Money* (The Big House); *Talking About A Revolution* (Tiata Fahodzi theatre company); *Hot in here* (Pigfoot Theatre company); *Yellowman* (Orange Tree Theatre); *When The Long Trick's Over*; *All of the conversations/Another fucking play about Race* (ArtsEd); *Athena* (The Yard); *STATEMENTS AFTER AN ARREST UNDER THE IMMORALITY* (Orange Tree Theatre); *Alice* (Landor_Space); *Invisible Light* (Tristan Bates Theatre); *Sad Girls* (Edinburgh Fringe); *Dana is her name* (audio comic, produced by Todd Bell & Stephanie Cotter).

Theatre503 is at the forefront of identifying and nurturing new voices at the very start of their careers and launching them into the industry. They stage more early career playwrights than any other theatre in the world – with over 120 writers premiered each year from festivals of short pieces to full length productions, resulting in employment for over 1,000 freelance artists through their year-round programme.

Theatre503 provides a diverse pipeline of talent resulting in modern classics like *The Mountaintop* by Katori Hall and *Rotterdam* by Jon Brittain – both Olivier Award winners – to future classics like Yasmin Joseph's *J'Ouvert*, winner of the 2020 James Tait Black Prize and transferred to the West End/BBC Arts and *Wolfie* by Ross Willis, winner of the 2020 Writers Guild Award for Best New Play. Writers who began their creative life at Theatre503 are now writing for the likes of *The Crown*, *Succession*, *Doctor Who*, *Killing Eve* and *Normal People* and every single major subsidised theatre in the country now boasts a new play by a writer who started at Theatre503.

Theatre503 Team

Artistic Director	Lisa Spirling
Interim Executive Director	Jules Oakshett
Literary Manager	Steve Harper
Producer	Ceri Lothian
General Manager	Tash Berg
Carne Associate Director	Jade Lewis
Literary Associate	Lauretta Barrow
Trainee Assistant Producers	Catherine Moriarty, Tsipora St. Clair Knights
Technical Manager	Misha Mah
Marketing Officer	Millie Whittam
Administrator	Lizzie Akita
Development Coordinator	Heloise Gillingham

Theatre503 Board

Erica Whyman OBE (Chair), Royce Bell (Co-Vice Chair), Eleanor Lloyd Emma Rees, Jack Tilbury, Luke Shires, Ollie Raggett, Roy Williams OBE Zena Tuitt

Our Supporters

Theatre503's work would not be possible without the support of the following individuals, trusts and organisations:

We are particularly grateful to Philip and Christine Carne and the long-term support of The Carne Trust for our International Playwriting Award, the 503 Five and Carne Associate.

503Patrons: Berlin Associates, Caroline & Tim Langton, Cas & Philip Donald, Catharine Roos, Céline Gagnon, David Baxter & Carol Rahn, DavidsonMorris Solicitors, Eilene Davidson, Eric Bensaude, Erica Whyman, Freddie Hutchins & Oliver Rawlins, Gaskell & Jennifer Jacobs, Geraldine Sharpe-Newton, Ian Mill KC, Jack Tilbury/Plann, Lisa Swinney, Lou Wilks & Tom Gowans, Louise Rawlins, Marcus Markou, Marianne Badrichani, Matthew Marren, Nick Hern Books, Pam Alexander & Roger Booker, Robert O'Dowd, Sean Winnett, Steve Winter, The Bell Family, The Bloor Family, Tim Willcox, United Agents and all our 503Friends and Share the Drama supporters.

503Slate Supporters: Cas & Philip Donald, Concord Theatricals, Eilene Davidson, Gordon Bloor, Jean Doumanian, Kater Gordon, Kofi Owusu Bempah, Royce Bell.

Arts Council England Grants for the Arts, Backstage Trust, Battersea Power Station Foundation (Right to Write), Cockayne Grants for the Arts (503 Productions), Concord Theatricals (503 Playwriting Award), Garrick Charitable Trust, Noel Coward Foundation (Rapid Write Response), Theatres Trust, The Foyle Foundation, The Orseis Trust (503Five), Wandsworth Borough Council, Wimbledon Foundation (Five-O-Fresh).

CHARACTERS

AMAN – 19 years old of West African descent (Nigeria)

HASSAN – 21 years old of West African descent (Nigeria) – **Aman's** older brother.

AIDAN BRADLEY – 19 years old male – White British

BILL BRADLEY – Middle-aged male, White British

LINTON HUGHES – Middle-aged male, White British

SETTING

Margate in Kent but the texture and feel reminiscent of coastal towns across the UK. The play flits between the Dalby Hotel and locations in the local community.

TIME

March 2015 in the run up to the UK general election.

AUTHOR'S NOTES

A dash (–) means a character being interrupted by another character.

The brothers Hassan and Aman often switch between English and pidgin English.

In memory of Daniel. A man of integrity and most importantly friendship, we miss you.

Scene One

(The sound of a bus pulling up, waves crashing against the sea and seagulls squawking. Brothers **HASSAN** *and* **AMAN** *have arrived in a coastal town in the UK, having been dispersed by the Home Office with minimal support. They cling to their backpacks, looking lost.* **HASSAN** *is searching on his phone, trying to find his bearings.)*

HASSAN. The next bus should come here.

(The bright neon lights of the arcade shine from across the road on the stage. The light spellbinds **AMAN**.)*

AMAN. Hassan look at it... I must go on dat rollercoaster!

HASSAN. How now? We have no money.

AMAN. I go find a way.

HASSAN. Aman, we no come here to play.

AMAN. One ride.

I will be five minutes.

HASSAN. Aman –

(Before **HASSAN** *can finish his sentence* **AMAN** *is running off like an excited teenager.)*

Be quick!

*(***HASSAN*** *is looking on at his brother from afar and trying to take in his new surroundings.)*

Before we leave

My mama go say

Look after your brudda

That bruddas

They are like two hands washing each other

Two parts of the same body

Connected for life

Like de tightest of fabrics

This is new to him

New to me

He is excited

But it is dangerous

Becoming refugees

Scattered seeds

A new community

    (**HASSAN** *takes a moment watching the people in the local community move about.*)

This new community...

A speck of black

In a sea of white faces

I've never go stand out so much

And

Want to be so hidden

    (*The sound of a bus pulling up and honking its horn.*)

Aman, we have to go.

The bus is here.

Aman!

> (**HASSAN** *is desperately trying to get* **AMAN***'s attention who is offstage.*)

Walahi I love my brother... but am I my brother's keeper?

Aman come on!

> (**AMAN** *races back.*)

AMAN. De guy no even let me enter through gate. But I swear I go go on dem next time. When I go, I go fly high in de air like Michael Jordan.

HASSAN. You no be serious. Just enter bus.

> (**AMAN** *puts his bag on and rushes offstage.* **HASSAN** *is looking back, wondering what lies in front of them.*)

Scene Two

(The Britannia pub Margate, **BILL**, **AIDAN** *and* **LINTON** *are sitting around a table putting the world to rights.)*

LINTON. Smash. They kick the door straight off the hinges.

AIDAN. Not even a knock?

LINTON. Couldn't hear. I was on the crapper upstairs.

BILL. Your IBS playing up again?

LINTON. Nah, just couldn't hear.

AIDAN. Police?

LINTON. That's what I'm thinking, but I'm clean as a whistle...

BILL. Or dodgy as a pair of Bangkok Rayban's.

AIDAN. You can't hold a man's past against him...

LINTON. "I've got a high court writ Mr Hughes... CCJ'S."

BILL. Told you.

AIDAN. CCJ'S?

BILL. County Court Judgement.

LINTON. Aaron... he's still registered at mine.

BILL. Thought you took him off ages ago?

LINTON. The benefits help cover the rent.

AIDAN. You tell 'em, he doesn't live there no more?

LINTON. Didn't wanna listen.

BILL. Heard they seize goods if you don't have the receipts.

AIDAN. How much does he owe?

LINTON. £5000.

BILL. £5000!

LINTON. Gambling debts… the casino.

BILL. All the Genting does is give people around here death and debt.

AIDAN. What'd they take?

(*Beat.*)

LINTON. Nothing! Pulled out a piece of paper… 'erm Mr. Hughes, we'll have to arrange a payment plan.'

AIDAN. What!

LINTON. Cos, there was fuck all of any value in the flat!

BILL. Bloody hell, you're a broke bastard.

LINTON. That's how I wanna go out of the world – free of possessions!

BILL. If that's the case, how about paying me back that fifty quid you owe me?

LINTON. It's better to give, than receive. Don't you remember our time with the Sally Army?

BILL. We volunteered there once and never went back!

LINTON. I'm trying to make penance while I can, give back to the community… always remember charity starts at home Aidan.

AIDAN. I know, I've been doing some bits with the volunteer service.

LINTON. Good man, cos before you know, you'll be an old codger like us. Wondering what you've done with your life and what comes next…

BILL. What's there to think about… you live and you die…

AIDAN. You think when you die that's it?

BILL. When I die, just cremate me and throw my ashes off the Harbour Wall. Simples.

LINTON. Well, at least you won't have to fork out for a horse-drawn carriage Aidan.

> (**AIDAN** *seems to be shaken by all this talk of death and is gripping onto a sketch book.*)

BILL. Top us up, Linton.

> (**LINTON** *returns to the bar and leaves the two men alone.*)

AIDAN. I'm going to head back.

BILL. You've only had one.

AIDAN. Got the morning shift.

BILL. There are no guests to tend to.

AIDAN. Just in case.

BILL. Come on, we're only getting started.

> (**AIDAN** *looks around the pub.*)

AIDAN. It's not my scene.

> (**BILL** *pulls* **AIDAN** *back by the arm.*)

BILL. I don't want you to feel you're on your own.

AIDAN. It's alright. I'm all good.

> (**BILL** *lets go of* **AIDAN**'s *arm, who takes one last look at the pub and his dad before leaving.* **LINTON** *wanders back over from the bar.*)

BILL. You had to mention death. What teenager wants to talk about death on a Friday night!

LINTON. And who makes their boy hang around with them on a Friday night? You two are tied at the hip. It isn't healthy. You need to give him some space to breathe.

BILL. What, so he can end up like your Aaron.

LINTON. If you keep a noose around the boy's neck, eventually he's going to hang himself.

BILL. Don't say that.

> (**BILL** *downs his pint, not wanting to contemplate the thought of losing* **AIDAN**.)

Scene Three

(A street corner outside of the local council building. Sound of busy passing traffic. **LINTON** *is hawking leaflets to locals without much luck.)*

LINTON. Invest in our young people and watch the difference we can make.

They are out of work and need to put their time to good use by helping us revamp our local spaces.

*(***LINTON*** *goes back to trying to hawk his leaflets when* **AMAN** *enters the stage with his backpack slung over his shoulder.)*

Service, not self, help our youngsters get off the streets and into employment.

*(***LINTON*** *turns his attention to* **AMAN** *and offers him a leaflet.)*

You interested?

AMAN. What?

LINTON. Get your hands dirty, getting into work.

AMAN. I'm not sure what you are saying?

*(***LINTON*** *takes the leaflet away from* **AMAN**.*)*

LINTON. Didn't think you would. You're new in town?

AMAN. Yeah...

LINTON. Thought I didn't recognise your face.

AMAN. There are many people in this town. I am sure you don't recognise everyone...

LINTON. Oh, no, me. I've got a photographic memory. Remember every face I do. So what are you doing here?

AMAN. I'm just hanging out.

LINTON. Not exactly a hotspot for youngsters round this part of town.

AMAN. Business… I have some business to take care of.

LINTON. On a street corner?

AMAN. *(Annoyed.)* My friend, can you please leave me alone.

LINTON. I'm just saying, it's not good for a man to loiter. Makes people feel uncomfortable.

AMAN. Is it any of your business what I do?

LINTON. Maybe. Maybe not. I'm just making friendly conversation. Getting to know you. Unless you got something to hide?

>   (**LINTON** *is pointing towards* **AMAN**'s *bag.*)

AMAN. Get out of here!

LINTON. Alright. Alright.

>   (**LINTON** *backs away seeing how agitated* **AMAN** *is.*)

I've never seen someone get so defensive about a bag.

AMAN. It's my personal belongings - I don't have to explain any ting to you. You're the most ridiculous man I have ever met.

>   (**AIDAN** *appears to the side of the stage.*)

LINTON. Ridiculous, who are you? You don't know who I am, what I do for this town. You're just a lazy delinquent.

AMAN. Don't talk down to me like that.

>   (**AIDAN** *intervenes as* **AMAN** *and* **LINTON** *are getting a bit too riled up.*)

AIDAN. Linton... are you harassing people again?

LINTON. If I don't look out for the community, who will?

> (**AIDAN** *is checking his phone and then looking at* **AMAN**.)

AIDAN. Aman?

I'm Aidan... the volunteer service matched us? I'm glad you made it.

> (**AIDAN** *puts his hand out for* **AMAN** *to shake, which he doesn't take.*)

AMAN. You know dis guy?

AIDAN. Sort of.

LINTON. Sort of? I've known you since you were in nappies.

> (**AMAN** *picks up his bag to leave.*)

AIDAN. Hold on.

AMAN. I didn't come to be wid people like dat.

AIDAN. He can be a little too enthusiastic.

AMAN. Enthusiastic... is that what you call it.

AIDAN. A nosey neighbour... every community has one.

> (*Silence.*)

Trust me.

AMAN. *(To* **LINTON**.*)* I want an apology.

LINTON. Then you'll be waiting a long time.

> (**AMAN** *bends down and picks up his bag.*)

AIDAN. Where are you going?

> (**AIDAN** *pulls him to the side for a chat.*)

AMAN. You tink after that, I want anything to do with you.

AIDAN. I'm supposed to be your mentor. Show you around... where's your brother?

AMAN. At de shops.

AIDAN. You got a lot of clothes in there. Where are you guys staying?

AMAN. In-between places...

AIDAN. You spoke to the council?

AMAN. I try...

AIDAN. System's complicated.

If you don't have a permanent address...

Look, me and my Dad run a hotel.

> (**AIDAN** *gets his sketch book out, writes on the pad, rips a page out and hands it to* **AMAN**.)

The address. You need anything, just pop in.

> (**AMAN** *takes his bag and leaves.*)

LINTON. I hope you ain't serious about that offer. He'll be more trouble than he's worth.

> (**AIDAN** *is shaking his head at* **LINTON***'s ignorance.*)

Scene Four

(The Dalby Hotel Margate. **BILL** *is clearing up plates after* **LINTON**'s *finished eating a full English breakfast.)*

BILL. You done with that?

LINTON. As much as my arteries can take. You can have the rest.

BILL. Nah I'm good, still on that diet.

Aidan's been showing me pictures of rotten colons getting me to stick to it.

I've gotta admit I feel more energetic.

Less bloated.

LINTON. Yeah, but at what cost?

(As **LINTON** *is texting on his phone.* **BILL** *looks over his shoulder and goes to take a sneaky bite of the sausage.)*

Oi! Thought you were on a diet?

BILL. I am but the grease, the salt. It's like a party's going on in my mouth.

*(***LINTON***'s phone is going off with notifications.* **LINTON** *is looking at his phone but appears lost by what he is seeing.)*

LINTON. I don't understand.

BILL. What?

LINTON. This Twitter thing.

*(***LINTON*** *hands* **BILL** *his phone.)*

BILL. You're too old for all this.

LINTON. It's Brenda's boy's idea.

BILL. Lewis?

What's he doing?

LINTON. The new Head of Comms for the party.

BILL. Pizza face.

Has he even started shaving yet?

LINTON. Meant to help with outreach – make us more modern.

BILL. Have you seen yourself – fifty old white blokes.

Your group picture looks like a *Status Quo* revival band.

Not a political party.

> (**BILL** *is looking through* **LINTON***'s twitter feed.*)

Why would you say that?

LINTON. What?

They were calling me gammon... pale, male and stale. How's that not offensive? I was just standing my ground.

BILL. They can ban you for that sort of thing.

LINTON. What for speaking my mind?

BILL. Take it down.

LINTON. No.

BILL. You've got people liking it.

LINTON. Because people want you to say it as it is.

They can see what's happening.

Cliftonville is unrecognisable these days.

Kids playing in Dalby Street and shouting at each other in twenty different languages.

It's a shithole.

Thanet council is a disgrace and I'm just giving a voice to it.

BILL. With that type of language?

LINTON. Says in my bio – views are my own.

(**BILL** *hands* **LINTON** *back his phone.*)

BILL. Your funeral.

LINTON. You can't be naïve about what we're up against.

BILL. Since we were kids, you've been a rabble-rouser.

Always looking to pick a fight.

LINTON. You had no problem when I stood up to Ashley Thompson. You might not like my tactics, but I get things done, produce results.

BILL. And this is your latest crusade...

LINTON. I'm standing up for what I believe in. Can you say the same?

BILL. I've got a business to run. My punters come from all walks of life.

LINTON. Profit over people.

Our kids around here have nothing to do. No business or industry for them to grow up and work in.

But we're changing all of that.

We've got them renovating the old crazy-golf course near the lido.

Turning it into a skate park.

Giving them something productive to do.

(**BILL** *gets up to clear his plate.*)

Look, what I'm saying is we have to invest in our communities and I'll expect the same sort of loyalty I've shown you over the years.

BILL. What? A free meal ticket?

You've already eaten me out of house and home.

(**BILL** *rubs* **LINTON**'*s stomach in jest.*)

LINTON. I'm serious mate.

Serious about the party.

Working my way up.

More serious about it than I've been about anything in my whole life.

I think I've found something that I'm good at... I care about.

BILL. Alright, I hear you. I need to clear the bins.

(**BILL** *pats* **LINTON** *on the back and goes to the back to clear the rubbish. He looks on from afar at* **LINTON**, *unsure of the journey his friend is venturing down.*)

Scene Five

*(The Dalby Hotel – **BILL** and **AIDAN** are cleaning and moving the furniture in the hotel's lobby.)*

AIDAN. How'd you wanna do this?

BILL. I'll take this side, you do the other half.

*(**AIDAN** is wiping down the surface with a cloth and some cleaning products.)*

You have to use bleach for that.

*(**BILL** hands **AIDAN** the bleach.)*

Put some elbow grease in it.

*(**BILL** is standing over **AIDAN** watching him scrub. **AIDAN** stops and turns to his father.)*

AIDAN. I'm good. I know what I'm doing.

BILL. Alright...

(Beat.)

Pub quiz next week. I put your name down.

AIDAN. What! Why?

BILL. We need the numbers.

(Beat.)

Thought it would be a laugh...

AIDAN. I'll do you a deal. I'll come if you get us a cleaner?

BILL. We can't afford it... No decent booking in a month and you're talking about hiring – you need your head sorting.

AIDAN. We need to get out there and get some new trade.

BILL. New trade... you don't get it. Your standard punter comes down for one of three things – a dirty weekend, family break or business trip.

AIDAN. That's your experience.

BILL. Exactly – experience. Which you don't have! Now get me the baking soda out of the cupboard upstairs.

> (**AIDAN** *is making his way offstage to the cupboard.*)

AIDAN. We need to diversify.

> (*We hear the door to the hotel creep open;* **AMAN** *and* **HASSAN** *enter.*)

BILL. There you go with those big words.

> (**BILL** *turns around to see* **HASSAN** *and* **AMAN** *standing there with their bags.*)

Can I help?

> (**HASSAN** *is looking at the paper in his hand.*)

HASSAN. Dalby hotel?

BILL. Yeah. Are you looking for a room?

HASSAN. Yes.

BILL. Check-in doesn't open for a couple of hours. Why don't you come back later?

> (**AIDAN** *comes out from the back.*)

These lads are looking for a room.

AIDAN. Well, you better book them in.

BILL. We're not open yet.

HASSAN. We can come back...

AIDAN. No, no, no. Come in.

(**AIDAN** *offers* **AMAN** *his hand acting like they haven't met before to* **AMAN**'s *surprise who plays along with it.* **BILL** *steps in to assert his authority.*)

BILL. Bill... Bill Bradley.

(**BILL** *offers his hand to* **AMAN** *which he shakes belatedly.*)

Your name. When we introduce ourselves, we share our name? So, what's yours son?

AMAN. Aman...

(**HASSAN** *steps in realising his brother isn't doing great introducing himself to* **BILL**.)

HASSAN. I'm Hassan.

BILL. *(To* **AMAN**.*)* That's a firm handshake – take note

AIDAN. Shall we get you checked in?

(**HASSAN** *digs his papers out of his bag. He's about to hand it to* **AIDAN** *when* **BILL** *steps in and takes it off of him.*)

BILL. What's this then?

(**BILL** *is reviewing the paperwork.*)

We don't take benefits.

(**AMAN** *and* **HASSAN** *are looking at each other unsure of what to do*)

AIDAN. We can sort it.

BILL. I don't trust it. I need a date to process the booking.

AIDAN. Just create an open booking, let me show you.

(**AIDAN** *makes his way over to the laptop.*)

BILL. I know how, but I can't guarantee I can hold the room indefinitely. So we're gonna have to sort these payment dates later.

HASSAN. OK.

> (**BILL** *is looking at the computer.*)

BILL. So you'll be sharing a double.

AMAN. We can't have our own rooms?

BILL. Not possible.

AIDAN. Dad – we've got the space.

BILL. Not at these prices, we can't go making exceptions.

> (*Silence.*)

HASSAN. Double is fine.

BILL. OK then. Breakfast is served from seven to ten a.m.

> (**BILL** *dangles the keys for* **AMAN** *to take, take before handing them over to* **HASSAN** *instead.*)

Few rules. No friends after ten. You can hang out with your mates outside.

HASSAN. No problem.

BILL. No hanky panky.

HASSAN. Hanky panky?

BILL. Sex.

AMAN. Agbaya.

HASSAN. Aman.

BILL. English... you have to speak English here.

> (*Silence.*)

The shower is just upstairs on the right; can be cold, but will help you adjust.

AMAN. Yes, sir.

> (**BILL** *turns around to hand the boys a couple of towels. When* **BILL** *has his back turned,* **AMAN** *takes the piss out of* **BILL***'s authority, standing in an armed salute.* **AIDAN** *finds it hilarious and the two lads have a wry smile and giggle.*)

BILL. Well, at least someone can make him laugh.

> (*Beat.*)

I take it you're not working yet?

> (*Beat.*)

The benefits... it's a trap.

I don't want people to think I'm housing scroungers. Aidan, make sure you get 'em down to the job centre or volunteering if they're not allowed to work.

> (**BILL** *retrieves a newspaper from behind his desk.*)

You can have a read of the jobs in this, to start yourself off. My family had little when we came over from Ireland but just look at me now. This is all self-made.

AIDAN. (*Laughs.*) What, you Alan Sugar now?!

BILL. Why don't you just show 'em the room?

> (**AIDAN** *leads* **AMAN** *and* **HASSAN** *upstairs.*)

AIDAN. I didn't think you would come.

AMAN. We had nowhere else to go...

(**BILL** *is left to sort out the rest of the booking
and is looking confused about how having
the boys as guests will work in the long run.*)

Scene Six

> (**HASSAN** *and* **AMAN** *are sitting on the floor playing cards.* **HASSAN** *lays the cards on the table and begins counting them.*)

HASSAN. *OK, watch em.*

> *Queen*
>
> *King*
>
> *Jack*
>
> *Ten*
>
> *Nine.*

I go finish you oh!

AMAN. OK. OK.

> (*Beat.*)

How work go be?

> (**AMAN** *picks up the cards he's been dealt.*)

HASSAN. It's work now.

AMAN. The people?

HASSAN. Albanian, Polish, British... some work hard, some don't.

> (**AMAN** *puts down a card.*)

That's two for mistake.

> (**AMAN** *picks up his card.*)

You go find something for yourself?

AMAN. Nobody go hire me now.

I go change my name, to one oyinbo name. Like... 'John Smith.'

HASSAN. Don't be stupid. Why don't you come chop with me now?

AMAN. It no go do em for me.

HASSAN. It no go do em for you. What go do for you den?

AMAN. I don't know.

HASSAN. You don't know. Ah. Aman.

(Beat.)

Did you go to the Western Union?

(Silence.)

Aman!

AMAN. It go close before I get there, now.

HASSAN. I no go trust you to do anyting –

AMAN. You're way too stressed, bro. You need to relax. Look at the lines on your forehead.

HASSAN. You lie! I no go have lines on my forehead.

AMAN. Grey hair.

HASSAN. Shut up your mout!

*(**AMAN** is examining his brother's hair.)*

AMAN. Walahi, I see some grey.

*(**HASSAN** is checking out his hair, using the camera on his phone.)*

You need to have fun. Get yourself a girlfriend.

*(**AMAN** puts his arm around his brother.)*

A beautiful girl, an English Rose. You can go out dancing together and she can help dye your grey hair!

HASSAN. Aman, you are funny... but I'm not here for fun. I'm here for de work, sabi?

(*Beat.*)

Make money... for Maryam... for Younas.

AMAN. That's you... I don't have kids... I'm sick of it. Money... it's all people back home care about!

HASSAN. It's not like that.

AMAN. When was the last time, they ask how bodi? Eh?

(*Beat.*)

They tink dis place is easy and you go make money, den we all go chop. Like that!

(**HASSAN** *clicks his fingers.*)

Why I go give my own to someone else?

HASSAN. Because...

AMAN. For where!

HASSAN. Because they have nutting!

AMAN. Then tell them to get on a boat and risk their lives for it! Eediots!

HASSAN. You forgot what Mama go do for you?

AMAN. Look, I know how it looks but I'm trying.

(**HASSAN** *puts the rest of his cards down.*)

HASSAN. Again you lose!

AMAN. You only wanted to play because you know I don't understand the rules!

HASSAN. Doesn't matter what we play, I always win.

AMAN. I dunno, you're getting kind of big. You used to be the fastest runner in the whole of our village.

Now you go get an uncle belly.

HASSAN. For where!

AMAN. Mo Farah... more like slow Farah.

HASSAN. I'm still stronger than you.

> (**HASSAN** *points to the floor for* **AMAN** *to get down into the press-up position.*)

AMAN. What, now?

> (**AMAN** *gets down and begins doing press-ups.*)

Why are you laughing?

HASSAN. The vein coming out of your head!

That's ten.

AMAN. What, I've done more!

> (**AMAN**'*s arms are shaking.*)

HASSAN. Fifteen.

AMAN. Thirty!

> (**AMAN**'*s arms are collapsing under the weight of his body.*)

HASSAN. Loser!

> (**HASSAN** *is in hysterics when* **BILL** *enters.* **BILL** *is not visible to him.*)

BILL. You're making too much noise.

> (**HASSAN** *turns around in shock to see* **BILL** *standing behind him.*)

You're disturbing the other guests.

HASSAN. We'll keep it down.

(**BILL** *looks around the room before leaving.*)

BILL. Good.

AMAN. You gonna fix the shower?

BILL. Excuse me.

AMAN. It leaks.

BILL. Fine when I checked it this morning, you break it?

AMAN. Why would I break it? The light doesn't work either.

BILL. When you signed the contents form, you flagged nothing.

AMAN. I thought the customer is always right?

BILL. You're not customers, you're –

AMAN. What? I know my rights and business is based on reviews.

BILL. You wouldn't dare.

(*Silence.*)

I'll check it in the morning.

AMAN. Good.

(**AMAN** *sees* **BILL** *towards the door and out of the room.*)

(*Silence.*)

HASSAN. All dis wahala.

AMAN. Because I speak up, it's a problem eh? This white man no go take you seriously till you show him pepper! Am I wrong?

HASSAN. Even when you're right, you're wrong.

AMAN. So say nothing and let him talk to us like that. No one controls me.

HASSAN. You think you know it all? So clever, but you don't have a job.

AMAN. I do.

HASSAN. Where now?

> *(Silence.)*

That's what I thought.

AMAN. I go get a job and chop more money in hour, than you go see in a day!

HASSAN. Rubbish. I go believe em when I see em.

> (**HASSAN** *goes to lie down.* **AMAN** *is fuming, wanting to prove himself.)*

Scene Seven

(**AIDAN** *is gardening, when* **AMAN** *is passing by and stops to watch what he is doing.* **AIDAN** *has his back turned to* **AMAN**, *so it appears as if he doesn't notice him.*)

AIDAN. It's not a museum.

(**AIDAN** *stares back at* **AMAN**.)

AMAN. Huh?

AIDAN. Staring and watching.

AMAN. Sorry.

(**AIDAN** *goes back to tending to the plants.*)

You're doing it wrong?

AIDAN. Excuse me?

AMAN. You're supposed to have more soil at the bottom.

AIDAN. I think I know what I'm doing.

(**AIDAN** *goes back to potting the plants, but* **AMAN** *shakes his head in irritation.*)

AMAN. No, no, no...

(**AMAN** *takes the plant from* **AIDAN**.)

Like dis. See... and then you fill in the plant.

(**AMAN** *hands the plant back to* **AIDAN** *and* **AMAN** *watches him whilst he plants it.*)

(*Sighs.*) No.

(**AMAN** *comes up behind* **AIDAN**, *takes his hands and shows how it is done.*)

Like this. Then you have to pat it.

AIDAN. OK. Thanks.

> (**AMAN** *lets go of* **AIDAN***'s hand.* **AMAN** *is rubbing his stomach.*)

AMAN. I've put on so much weight since I come to dis country... it's the shiken and ships.

AIDAN. Chicken and chips?

AMAN. That's what I said.

> (*Silence.*)

AIDAN. Your brother out?

AMAN. Yeah.

You can go a little crazy when you have nothing to do.

AIDAN. Town is quiet this time of year.

> (**AMAN** *is wandering around the garden.*)

Look, this job is gonna take me forever and I still need to do the stock take.

You wanna help?

AMAN. Err yeah.

> (**AMAN** *takes off his jacket.*)

AIDAN. I can't pay you much.

AMAN. It's OK.

AIDAN. You sure?

AMAN. Yeah.

AIDAN. Alright start on that side.

> (**AMAN** *is tending to some plants on the stage.*)

You've done this before...

AMAN. My grandfada was a farmer.

> (**AMAN** *is crouching as he looks up at the clear sky and listens to the sound of starlings flying and the water crashing against the shore.*)

This place isn't bad.

AIDAN. The town might be run down, but you can't beat the sight..

> (*Beat.*)

AMAN. Aidan... I never said thank you for helping us to find a place to stay.

AIDAN. It's OK ...it worked out best for everyone.

AMAN. I wasn't sure about it at first. I mean, when I first met you, I thought you were one of them. Looking at us like we're nothing. And I didn't think after that thing in the street... I know you said you'd help... but you came through.

> (**AMAN** *holds his hand out for* **AIDAN** *to shake.*)

AIDAN. I'm just trying to do my bit.

AMAN. Where do you go out with your friends around here?

Because I can't find anything to do.

AIDAN. I don't go out much.

AMAN. That is why you volunteer... to make friends?

AIDAN. My thera... I was told it would help me meet people.

AMAN. Oh.

(Silence.)

You like to dance, listen to music?

*(**AIDAN** looks at his watch.)*

AIDAN. We should finish this.

AMAN. We should go out, listen to music.

AIDAN. You're our guest... it's not professional...

AMAN. You sound like my case worker.

*(**AMAN** comes up close to **AIDAN**.)*

Saturday?

AIDAN. I'm working till ten.

AMAN. Perfect, the real fun doesn't start till later.

(Silence.)

Come on, what you say. Work hard, play harder...

AIDAN. Maybe if you get this done...

*(**AMAN** gets back to work on potting the plants. As he does so, he and **AIDAN** give each a smile as they tuck into their work.)*

Scene Eight

(**HASSAN** *is in a queue in the local Lidl holding a shopping basket when* **BILL** *comes up behind him.*)

BILL. Big queue...

(**HASSAN** *looks back but doesn't say anything to him.* **BILL** *peers into* **HASSAN**'s *shopping basket.*)

BILL. They're not ripe.

HASSAN. Sorry.

BILL. They're no good.

Still green.

Will take a week for them to ripen.

(**BILL** *is peering into* **HASSAN**'s *shopping basket.*)

Got a lot of snacks in there.

HASSAN. A few.

BILL. Hope you're not eating that in your room.

I had a punter that would eat all sorts of crap in his room.

Would leave a right mess.

Ended up getting mice.

Had to serve him notice.

They tried to tell me I couldn't evict him because he had mental health problems.

Asperger's, I think they called it.

He was a nice enough lad.

A little erratic...

What I'm saying is that we don't want a problem with rodents...

HASSAN. You had mice?

BILL. Don't tell me a big lad like you fears a little mouse?

HASSAN. I don't like em.

> (**BILL** *is still following* **HASSAN** *around the store.*)

BILL. I love Lidl.

Their packaging looks like cheap tat but their baked goods are quality.

Try this.

> (**BILL** *offers* **HASSAN** *a piece of a croissant.*)

HASSAN. But you haven't paid for it?

BILL. Call it a sample.

> (**HASSAN** *looks around before taking the croissant from* **BILL** *and eating it.*)

Bellissima.

HASSAN. Bismillah

BILL. No bellissima, it's Italian.

HASSAN. Sorry, but before we eat, we say Bismillah

BILL. I don't know about that mumbo jumbo.

> (**BILL** *moves down the aisle.* **HASSAN** *feels compelled to follow him now as if they are both shopping together.*)

My ex wouldn't have been caught dead in Lidl.

HASSAN. Ex?

BILL. Ex-wife.

She would've killed me if she knew where I was shopping.

She was all about the brands, the names you know.

Would call her Mrs. M&S.

Everything she owned/would buy would be from that shop.

Curtains, clothes, food – you name it.

> (**BILL** *bends down to pick up the shopping and his back gives way.*)

BILL. Ooh.

HASSAN. You OK?

BILL. Yeah all good.

> (**BILL** *is clearly in a lot of pain.*)

HASSAN. Cos if you're not, you can just say?

BILL. Nah, nah, you're alright.

> (**HASSAN** *steps in to help him and support him onto a stool.*)

BILL. Thanks. I think it's gone.

> (**BILL** *is moving around the stool attempting to get comfortable.*)

HASSAN. You OK?

BILL. Just give me a minute.

HASSAN. Why doesn't Aidan do the shopping if you've got a bad back?

BILL. He tries but all of this hotel business doesn't come natural to him.

Got his head in the clouds.

Dreaming half the time.

> (**BILL** *looks* **HASSAN** *up and down.*)

Why are you dressed like that?

> (**BILL** *is pointing to* **HASSAN***'s shabby look of beaten-up trainers and gym wear.*)

HASSAN. I like to run.

Every morning.

Five miles.

BILL. Five miles?

HASSAN. Yes, five miles.

BILL. How long does it take you?

HASSAN. I don't know… twenty two minutes.

BILL. Rubbish.

HASSAN. Walahi.

I leave the hotel at seven.

I come back at seven twenty two a.m.

BILL. Every time?

HASSAN. All the time.

What?

BILL. It's just a very quick time.

HASSAN. I've always been fast.

Fastest in my school.

Fastest in my village.

They call me Forest.

Like the man in the movie.

BILL. Forrest Gump?

HASSAN. Yes. I just keep on running.

BILL. And running.

And running.

I love that film.

You think you're Forrest Gump?

This your 'British' Dream?

HASSAN. I come to work hard.

He was nobody.

No one believed in him.

Helped him.

But he makes it.

Make it to the top.

BILL. It's a movie.

HASSAN. I know this.

But if you work hard, you can do it.

BILL. You've got a positive attitude.

(Silence.)

I used to run.

Back in the day.

Long-distance.

10,000 metres...

I was good.

Could've been one of the best.

I used to love to train.

My friends would hate it but not me, every day I would
wake up and be ready.

The burn after a workout – that was my drug.

The grind through winter.

HASSAN. You win?

>   (**BILL** *lifts his trouser leg.*)

BILL. Cruciate ligament.

My knee blew out.

They couldn't do the surgeries they do now, back then. Changed my whole life just like that, it did.

Trained up in the hotel with my Dad and been doing that ever since.

Would do anything to run again.

Feel the wind on my back.

Wipe the sweat from my brow.

You're a lucky young man.

HASSAN. You come with me – you show me how to go faster.

BILL. I haven't gotten involved in it for years.

HASSAN. You help me?

>   (*Silence.*)

BILL. They say those who can't do, teach.

seven a.m you say?

HASSAN. Yes.

BILL. Be there sharp as I don't take prisoners.

HASSAN. Yes sir.

>   (**BILL** *holds his hand out and* **HASSAN** *shakes it*)

Scene Nine

(**AIDAN** *is sitting at reception, he is sketching on his pad when* **BILL** *enters.* **AIDAN** *hides his drawing pad and pretends to be focused on the laptop.*)

BILL. Aid gives us a hand with this for a second.

(**AIDAN** *goes over and helps* **BILL** *turn the table on its side.*)

Been meaning to fix this for a while, it's always been unstable. Does my head in.

(**BILL** *notices the laptop open.*)

How are the books looking?

AIDAN. Yeah good.

BILL. Let me have a look.

AIDAN. I'm still logging in.

(**BILL** *leaves working on the table and makes his way over to* **AIDAN** *who has the laptop on his lap.*)

I don't get how you just put everything online, where does it all go?

AIDAN. A cloud.

BILL. And where's that cloud?

AIDAN. I dunno.

BILL. So you don't even know where it's stored?

AIDAN. Everything is like that – email, banking, documents...

BILL. I prefer the old-fashioned way where you keep hold of your receipts and file your taxes before the end of the year.

AIDAN. You'll get used to it.

BILL. Let me see it then.

AIDAN. I'm still logging in.

>   (**BILL** *goes into his back pocket and brings out a letter.*)

BILL. This came addressed to you today... Central Saint Martins college?

>   (**AIDAN** *gets up and takes the brochure from* **BILL**.)

What's that then?

AIDAN. More junk mail.

BILL. You thinking of going back to college?

AIDAN. No, they probably just got my name from some database. I get them all the time.

BILL. First one I've seen.

Might not do you harm going back to college?

AIDAN. What? Do you think so?

BILL. Yeah.

AIDAN. Because I was thinking –

BILL. Food hygiene

I wanted to put you on a course.

AIDAN. What?

BILL. That punter who got food poisoning a couple of months ago... we haven't had a booking in weeks.

AIDAN. That wasn't me.

BILL. The eggs.

AIDAN. Past their sell-by date.

BILL. Not if you cook 'em properly.

> (**AIDAN** *has finished logging into the online accounting system, he pushes the laptop over to* **BILL** *to have a look.*)

That's clever.

AIDAN. It's got cash flow and revenue from the last five years; if you just click here.

BILL. Bloody hell.

It's different when you see it like that. I knew we were doing badly but fuck me...

AIDAN. But look at this. In the last month since we took the boys on. We've made much more.

BILL. That's not bad.

AIDAN. If we did some more –

BILL. We can't.

AIDAN. But you just said.

> (**BILL** *closes the laptop.*)

BILL. I'm into hospitality, not homelessness.

> (**AIDAN** *takes back the laptop.*)

I want you to see this place for what it is.

The heritage.

The history.

We can't turn it into a youth hostel.

AIDAN. It was just an idea.

(**BILL** *returns to fixing his table, while* **AIDAN** *types away on the laptop.*)

BILL. You OK to cover the evening shift tomorrow?

Linton's Missus has invited me over for dinner.

AIDAN. I can't

BILL. You've got plans?

(*Beat.*)

Sorry I didn't mean it like that. Any chance you can shift 'em?

AIDAN. Don't think so.

(*Silence.*)

BILL. Must be important...

AIDAN. Just going out...

(*Beat.*)

What?

BILL. Nothing, it's good for a young lad like you to be out and about.

(*Beat.*)

Whatever it is, it's made you more...

Engaged

(*Beat.*)

You know it's alright if you want to have someone over.

Like I know you think I'm...

AIDAN. There's no one to bring home.

BILL. But if there was I think I'd be alright with it.

(**BILL** *tries to turn the table back over and* **AIDAN** *moves to give him a hand.*)

Much more steady that.

AIDAN. Looks good.

(**AMAN** *comes through the entrance and* **BILL** *stops in his tracks looking at him.*)

AMAN. Morning.

AIDAN. Morning.

(**AMAN** *heads upstairs.* **AIDAN** *is watching his every move and staring at* **AMAN** *a bit too long for* **BILL***'s liking.*)

BILL. You wanna help me put this stuff back?

(**BILL** *and* **AIDAN** *are putting the table back in its original place.*)

How are you getting on with him?

AIDAN. Alright.

BILL. His brother is a nice lad.

AIDAN. I haven't spoken to him much.

BILL. You know this is temporary?

AIDAN. I know.

(*Silence.*)

BILL. I just don't want you getting too attached...

(**BILL** *puts an arm around* **AIDAN***'s shoulder.*)

You're in good space.

I know with your mum not being around and your college course not working out...

AIDAN. Dad. I'm good.

BILL. I'm just saying if you need to talk.

AIDAN. I've got my therapist.

BILL. You are taking your medication right?

AIDAN. Every night and sleeping well.

BILL. Good.

AIDAN. I'm fine.

Trust me.

BILL. I just don't want to see you in a bad place again.

> (**BILL** *has his arm around* **AIDAN**, *who looks rather guilty.*)

Scene Ten

(**HASSAN** *comes into the bedroom, sweaty after a run and a training session with* **BILL**. **AMAN** *is lounging around on his phone and looking at different things that he wants to buy online.*)

AMAN. I didn't hear you leave this morning.

HASSAN. I didn't wanna wake you.

AMAN. I don't know how you do it waking up that early, it's not normal.

HASSAN. Not normal? Normal people don't sleep past ten.

AMAN. Not me. I need my twelve hours of beauty sleep.

HASSAN. Twelve hours! Eediot.

(**HASSAN** *throws his smelly t-shirt at this brother.*)

AMAN. Bro that stinks.

(*He throws it back at* **HASSAN**, *who catches it and rubs the sweat on* **AMAN**.)

HASSAN. That is the smell of hard work. I need to rub it off on my lazy brother.

AMAN. Get off. That's disgusting.

HASSAN. Not to me. There's nothing like a good run.

And I'm getting faster. Better. Like how I used to be.

(**HASSAN** *is showing off his muscles.*)

Looking and feeling good.

AMAN. Who has turned you into de terminator? This robot.

HASSAN. Mr Bill now. You know he used to be an athlete...

AMAN. De old baba, wid de grey hair.

HASSAN. Yes now.

AMAN. He go have heart attack when he step on de track.

HASSAN. You laugh but he go coach me. I go run faster den ever before. Go get me to enter the local half marathon.

AMAN. So you go love Mr Bill now?

HASSAN. I no go say dat but you should come with me. See for yourself.

AMAN. I'm busy.

HASSAN. Busy?

AMAN. Yeah.

HASSAN. Busy scratching your ass and picking your nose.

AMAN. Must you tink so little of me?

HASSAN. Have you given me a reason not too?

AMAN. Maybe not... but I haven't caused any trouble either which is good, no?

(**HASSAN** *is stretching.*)

But I'm a little bit broke at the moment.

HASSAN. Mr "I go chop more money than you" has no cash!

AMAN. I don't why you make fun of me. How you can be so happy dressing and living like this.

HASSAN. Living like this? As if you are de King of England used to living in Buckingham Palace.

AMAN. You wouldn't understand, you have no swag...

HASSAN. Swag? Ah. Why you tink Maryam, go marry me? My shoes be so shiny she go see her face in dem.

AMAN. Talking about shiny shoes – are you twenty one or a forty-year-old man... It's about de latest trainers... Jordan's... Yeezy's...

HASSAN. And how you go get that?

AMAN. With a little investment from you?

HASSAN. Kai... you go lose your mind... oh... You know how hard I work for that money.

I'm not putting my neck on the line so you can go out galavanting.

AMAN. Bro come on. It's something important to me.

HASSAN. What is it?

AMAN. I can't say.

HASSAN. You can't say but want my money. Want to joke with me but never tell me what you're up to? Won't take an interest in what I do.

AMAN. Alright I'll come to your race – just lend me some money?

HASSAN. You promise you'll come?

AMAN. I'll even hold a sign up for you OK?

HASSAN. OK good and where are you going that you need money? Want to get dressed up for?

AMAN. Just out, I need this man. I'm not like you, I can't just do the things you do. I need to live and be around people doing stuff. I'm a social guy.

HASSAN. Well you go have to learn to make your own. I'm not your Daddy and I no go let you waste my money. I go have a shower.

(**HASSAN** *leaves to go to shower but does a doubles take and decides to give* **AMAN** *the money after all.*)

AMAN. I love you but you still stink though!

Scene Eleven

(The sound of high tempo music increases. We see the blaring and bright lights of Margate's Dreamland theme park in the background. **AMAN** *comes running onto the stage with* **AIDAN** *behind him.)*

AMAN. Come on let's go on it.

AIDAN. I don't like heights.

AMAN. Live a little.

(The two men pull two chairs into the centre of the stage and enjoy the simulated experiences of a roller coaster. They move and shake with every jolt of the ride.)

Wohoooo!

AIDAN. I can't look.

I'm going to die.

Oh my God.

(They both have their arms raised in the air in a thrill of ecstasy, before jolting as if the ride has come to a halt. **AMAN** *grabs* **AIDAN**'s *hand.)*

AMAN. Come on, let's get out of here.

(The lighting on stage gets a bit darker like dim street lighting. The sound of the ocean can be heard crashing against the beach as the tide comes in and drunken revellers can be heard in the background as it gets quieter as we move into the scene. **AIDAN** *is trying to keep a close eye on him.)*

The noise, the lights, the DJ!

> (**AMAN** *turns to* **AIDAN** *and holds his hand.*)

Awww the DJ!

AIDAN. He was pretty good.

AMAN. He was amazing! When he played that last tune, my God!

> (**AMAN** *takes* **AIDAN**'s *hand and starts dancing with him.*)

AIDAN. What are you doing?

> (**AIDAN** *stops embarrassed.*)

(*Laughs.*) You're off your tits.

AMAN. No, I'm just free!

You've got to enjoy life.

It's what I keep telling my brother.

Relax – have fun.

You had fun, right?

AIDAN. Yeah, it was a laugh.

AMAN. Where to next?

AIDAN. Let's just chill here.

> (**AMAN** *looks out at the beach and the water.*)

AMAN. Food. How about we get food?

AIDAN. Later.

> (**AIDAN** *takes a seat.*)

Can we sit?

(The sound of water battering against the rocks makes **AMAN** *shift about nervously.)*

You alright?

AMAN. Yeah, I'm good...

AIDAN. I'm glad I came out.

AMAN. I had to drag you.

AIDAN. I'm not really one for noise and parties.

AMAN. And I try to be the life of the party. You know they say opposites attract.

*(***AMAN*** nudges ***AIDAN*** gently.)*

AIDAN. I don't know if I can keep up with your speed?

AMAN. I just try to appreciate life after everything I've seen. If you had experienced that, you'd do the same.

(Silence.)

Why were you so keen on helping me?

(Beat.)

AIDAN. 'Help yourself by helping others.'

It's what the posters said at the volunteer centre...

AMAN. You need help too?

AIDAN. I dunno... I guess we all do.

That we're all fucked up.

AMAN. I hear that.

AIDAN. We fuck each other up.

(Silence.)

AMAN. That's how you see it?

AIDAN. That's what life's shown me.

That you're on your own when it comes down to it.

AMAN. I don't believe that.

>(**AMAN** *stands up.*)

Come on.

Turn around.

AIDAN. What you gonna do?

AMAN. Just turn around.

>(**AIDAN** *eventually agrees to turn around, with his back to* **AMAN**.)

I want you to fall back.

AIDAN. Fuck off.

AMAN. Trust me.

AIDAN. I'm gonna fall.

AMAN. I'll catch you.

>(*Beat.*)

Come on.

>(**AIDAN** *closes his eyes, counts to five underneath his breath and falls backward.* **AMAN** *catches him breaking his fall and* **AIDAN** *is laying in his arms.*)

See I got you.

>(*As* **AMAN** *is helping* **AIDAN** *up they are facing each other, both breathing heavily and looking deeply into each other's eyes. It's an intimate, tense and warm moment.*)

Scene Twelve

(**BILL** *and* **LINTON** *are in the lobby of the Dalby hotel having a drink.* **LINTON** *is pacing back and forth; pensive.* **BILL** *is reading a paper.*)

LINTON. David Cameron's losing the plot, has no clue what people around here need but trumpets statements like an Emperor from his Westminster Palace.

BILL. That's politics for you... why I stay clear.

LINTON. I get your point but we can make real change locally, in this election. The local parliamentary candidate is thinking about packing it in with the Independence Party. Opens up a spot...

BILL. Been the same bloke for the past thirty years. I'll believe it when I see it.

LINTON. Jean Henderson who runs the local bookies is giving it the talk of launching a bid. Jean – can you imagine that?

BILL. She'd be awful.

LINTON. I've been telling everyone that but they are thinking of supporting her.

BILL. The woman's stubborn as a bull. Saw her throw a geezer out once with her bare hands. Tough nut she is.

LINTON. Says she'll fight tooth and nail for it.

(**LINTON** *leans in.*)

Listen. I was thinking about going in for it but I'd have to declare this week. Would you support me?

(*Silence.*)

BILL. I'm not even a party member. Besides, I already told you that business and politics don't mix.

LINTON. Successful business owner, you're the perfect endorsement.

BILL. I don't know about the successful part.

LINTON. You don't give yourself enough credit mate. I remember when you'd be booked up six months in advance.

BILL. That was back in the day when you'd have to wait an hour to get into the arcade. The beach would be so packed that you couldn't even find space to set up a deck chair.

LINTON. Be standing outside the Britannia with a pint cos there were no seats inside.

> (*Silent.*)

Still, you're busy right? Picking up the hipster trade?

BILL. Nope.

LINTON. When they built the Turner Gallery, they promised the artsy-fartsy types would stream down from London.

BILL. Yeah, well...

> (**AIDAN** *walks in.*)

LINTON. How's it going son?

AIDAN. Yeah, alright. Hot waters gone?

> (**BILL** *is exasperated by hearing about the fault with the hot water.*)

LINTON. Margate wouldn't be Margate, without lads like you.

AIDAN. What do you want, Linton?

LINTON. Moi? Nothing, just happy to see you.

> (**AIDAN** *removes* **LINTON***'s arm from his shoulder.*)

AIDAN. Because when you've got that grin on your face you're usually scheming.

LINTON. You think so little of me.

BILL. Is he wrong?

LINTON. Alright... fundraising...

BILL. I knew it. What for?

LINTON. For the election.

AIDAN. You?

LINTON. Try not to act too surprised.

BILL. I thought you were just thinking about it.

LINTON. Actively.

BILL. You're canvassing.

LINTON. I'd call it community engagement.

BILL. Spoken like a true politician, you're getting good at this Linton.

LINTON. I'll take that as a compliment.

AIDAN. How much?

LINTON. Ten grand.

BILL. Ten grand!

LINTON. Things are competitive these days.

Campaign materials, staff – it ain't cheap. Rome wasn't built in a day.

AIDAN. But Margate was!

LINTON. That's just it – were a joke, a national joke. We need a vision for the town.

> (**LINTON** *hands* **AIDAN** *and* **BILL** *flyers.*)

AIDAN. You our visionary?!

LINTON. Oh ye of little faith. I've got big plans.

BILL. Yeah, think Harrods but with a Primark budget.

LINTON. If the community pulls together...

BILL. Who's got that kind of money?

LINTON. Remember 'service not self!'

Just look at the work we've begun last week on the skate park...

BILL. I've been meaning to get down there and check it out.

LINTON. The boys I've recruited are gonna put their blood, sweat and tears into that place.

It's a tragedy what's happening in our town and the only way we can change it is by rolling our sleeves up.

We've got to do something about it.

BILL. Look mate I wish we could help.

LINTON. Yes could by –

> (**AMAN** *comes on stage listening to music on his earphones and humming a tune interrupting them. Distracted, he's confronted by* **LINTON**'s *presence.*)

LINTON. Think you've taken a wrong turn son.

> (**AMAN** *takes out his earphones.*)

AMAN. Don't think so. This is where I live...

(**LINTON** *is looking at* **BILL** *confused as to why he would take in such a guest.*)

BILL. They're customers, came to us… we couldn't afford to turn away business.

LINTON. Came to you?

(**LINTON** *turns towards* **AIDAN** *looking for answers.*)

AIDAN. Dad, you need to fix the hot water.

BILL. I'm on it…

(**BILL** *heads offstage to fix the water.*)

LINTON. How'd you get them in here? And how are they affording? I know the government doesn't give them much.

AIDAN. It's business and we need business.

(**LINTON** *hands* **AIDAN** *a form.*)

LINTON. Well since we're talking business…

(**AIDAN** *reluctantly takes form.*)

LINTON. Good man… I'll expect to see you come good on your offer.

(**LINTON** *heads off, leaving* **AIDAN** *with an unwanted donation form in his hand.*)

Scene Thirteen

(**AIDAN** *is sitting in the dark at reception with only a small lamp giving him a little light. He has a blister pack of medication in his hand, pops two pills and downs the glass of water in front of him. He goes back to sketching in his notebook when he is startled by the sound of someone falling over. He puts away his notebook and pills to check out what's going on.*)

AMAN. Shit.

AIDAN. Aman?

(**AMAN** *appears out of the shadows of the darkness.*)

AMAN. Sorry.

AIDAN. What are you doing?

AMAN. I didn't want to wake anybody up.

AIDAN. You been out?

(*Beat.*)

AMAN. Just a little thing.

AIDAN. Right.

AIDAN. So what was it?

AMAN. Nothing big, just some of the other brothers from overseas.

AIDAN. Oh, that's good that you're... making friends.

AMAN. I wasn't sure if it would be your thing?

AIDAN. My thing?

AMAN. This morning you were acting like you didn't know me, with your Dad?

AIDAN. Things are delicate.

AMAN. If you say so.

> (**AMAN** *moves to go upstairs.*)

AIDAN. I had a good time the other night.

AMAN. I did too... but you're hard to read though Aidan.

Like, what's up with you sitting in the dark?

AIDAN. It's peaceful down here.

AMAN. Can I?

AIDAN. Yeah.

> (**AMAN** *sees* **AIDAN**'s *sketchbook on the table.*)

AMAN. What's that?

AIDAN. It's just a book.

AMAN. I know but what's in it?

AIDAN. Drawings and stuff.

AMAN. Can I see?

> (**AIDAN** *pauses before handing the book to* **AMAN**.)

You draw birds.

AIDAN. Starlings, the ones you see by the Harbour Wall.

They move in motion.

In sync, not one falls out of line.

The first one follows the patterns of the second.

And so on.

Then they make a vibration which is sent from the back to the front.

Formation.

AMAN. You are talented. Who teaches you?

> *(Silence.)*

AIDAN. Myself.

AMAN. Someone must have shown you?

AIDAN. I don't know it just comes to me naturally.

AMAN. I don't think Mr. Bill can do this!

AIDAN. No.

My Mum…

She died a couple of years ago. We used to sit in silence and just paint together.

Was our thing.

AMAN. It's good you're drawing again then?

> *(**AMAN** is rifling through **AIDAN**'s notebook.)*

Is that me?

> *(**AIDAN** snatches the drawing away from **AMAN**.)*

AIDAN. No, it's not.

AMAN. You're drawing me.

AIDAN. I said it's not.

AMAN. I saw it, show me!

AIDAN. You saw nothing.

AMAN. Why did you draw me like that?

My face is sad.

*(**AIDAN** turns around to look at **AMAN**.)*

AIDAN. It was when you were sitting alone, eating.

You were in the room by yourself and I was passing by.

The image just stayed in my head.

I had to draw it.

(Silence.)

Get it out of my head.

*(**AMAN** and **AIDAN** stare at each other, recognising one another's pain.)*

I gotta go get some sleep. I'm on the early shift.

*(**AMAN** grabs **AIDAN**'s hand to pull him back.)*

AMAN. This is it.

This is what you love doing.

The Art.

Your dream.

AIDAN. Dreams are for those who are sleeping and not awake to real life.

AMAN. So wake up and do what you want to do.

*(**AMAN** is pointing around the hotel.)*

AIDAN. Turn off the lights when you're done.

AMAN. Aidan, tomorrow night, eight p.m. in the park.

AIDAN. What?

AMAN. No questions, just be there.

*(**AIDAN** walks off, leaving **AMAN** a solitary figure in the hotel's lobby.)*

Scene Fourteen

*(**BILL** and **HASSAN** are walking and talking along the Margate Harbour Wall, **HASSAN** is in his running kit having just competed in the half marathon.)*

BILL. It's too early to say if you can make the leap to the top flight.

But this is a good first step, you took minutes off your PB.

I think 10,000 metres is your race – suits your kick at the end.

Left them for dead

*(**BILL** playfully punches **HASSAN** on the arm.)*

Shades of Ovett

Coe.

HASSAN. Who?

BILL. The greats.

Great Britons.

*(**HASSAN** shakes his head lost.)*

Coe's stride and technique made running look effortless.

He floated above the track, more than anyone I've witnessed.

His shoulders and trunk always looked relaxed, torso was one eighty degrees to the track, with no movement in the head.

Others might have had a beautiful stride, but they would lean forward, which isn't ideal.

Watching you today.

You've got real heart!

But you've got to be smarter.

Long-distance is all about strategy.

You can't just be impetuous and run fast.

You've gotta think.

>   (**BILL** *points towards his brain.*)

HASSAN. When I'm racing, I try to forget about all my problems until I finish.

Not allow any thoughts to come into my head.

Otherwise, my legs will fail me.

My speed will go down.

I clear my head.

Then it's just rhythm.

My mind

My body.

It's all one.

One machine.

Till I cross the line.

BILL. Nice.

HASSAN. Did you see the reporter at the end?

BILL. No.

HASSAN. He asked for my picture.

I let him take it.

Then he's asking me questions.

Where do you come from?

Why are you here?

I'm thinking – I just won the race.

You do not even ask me about my race.

Why does it matter where I'm from?

BILL. Cos no one's heard of you. When we entered you into the race at the last minute and you won out of nowhere. It's a great story.

HASSAN. But the people cheer for me.

Run...

Run...

Run faster.

BILL. People love an underdog.

Seeing someone triumph against the odds.

When they see you running, they see it like you're working.

Putting back in.

Applying yourself.

HASSAN. I do that every day.

That's what I don't understand.

When they see me in town they ignore me?

Pretend like I don't exist.

But you see me now?

Suddenly, I'm not invisible to you anymore?

(Silence.)

BILL. What have you been up to in town these past few weeks?

*(**BILL** holds his hands up in innocence.)*

I won't say a word, scouts honour.

(Silence.)

HASSAN. Nothing...

BILL. You sure? Cus when I was down the pub there was some rumbling amongst traders. Not happy about their labouring jobs being taken away. Wages are being undercut.

(Silence.)

HASSAN. You told me to find out if I can work. Once they tell me I can't. I keep my head down like you told me to do...

BILL. Good cos without your papers it's not legal... I wouldn't want to report it if I found something out... Besides, you're already getting benefits.

HASSAN. It's not much.

BILL. You're a single lad, roof over your head. What more do you need?

HASSAN. For my family... I send money back home.

*(**HASSAN** hands **BILL** a picture.)*

BILL. What's this?

HASSAN. My son.

BILL. How old?

HASSAN. Two.

*(**BILL** is inspecting the picture.)*

BILL. He's got your eyes.

HASSAN. He looks more like his mother.

*(**BILL** hands **HASSAN** back the picture.)*

BILL. Wife?

HASSAN. Yeah.

> *(Silence.)*

BILL. I was married around your age.

A lot of responsibility to have a family.

HASSAN. It is but I enjoy it so much.

> *(**HASSAN** is looking down at the photo of his son.)*

BILL. Look, forget all the outside noise, the reporters and the town.

Just focus on your running.

You're good at your running.

You and me, we couldn't be any more opposite.

But this.

This…

This is good.

> *(**HASSAN** picks up his sports bag and slings it over his shoulder, he shakes **BILL**'s hand.)*

We keep training.

We keep doing this.

We keep on winning.

> *(**HASSAN** nods in acceptance.)*

Scene Fifteen

(**AMAN** *has cleared out a secluded area, he's used fairy lights to illuminate the dark. He has laid down a mat with food and drink, creating a romantic setting.* **AIDAN** *is stumbling around trying to find* **AMAN**.)

AIDAN. This place doesn't even show up on my phone.

AMAN. Just through here.

AIDAN. I think something has bitten me.

(**AIDAN** *makes his way through and stumbles upon* **AMAN**'s *surprise*.)

Wow.

AMAN. You like it?

AIDAN. Yeah.

(**AMAN** *pours* **AIDAN** *a drink*.)

I haven't been here since I was a boy.

AMAN. I walk here sometimes when I want quiet.

You said you like quiet.

Sit, I want to show you something.

(**AMAN** *ushers for* **AIDAN** *to sit down*.)

In our culture we like to eat together.

AIDAN. I dunno if I can do this.

AMAN. See like this.

(**AMAN** *is showing* **AIDAN** *how to eat the food*.)

AIDAN. You made this?

What's that? Like a cooked banana?

AMAN. Oh you oyinbo people.

It's plantain.

Taste it.

AIDAN. That's nice, that is.

>(**AIDAN** *takes a bite of the plantain chips before pointing to the other bits of food.*)

What's that?

AMAN. Kilishi and chin chin.

>(**AIDAN** *is trying the food for the first time and is making a mess of it.*)

AIDAN. What?

AMAN. You couldn't eat more like a white guy – if you tried.

AIDAN. I've never eaten this before.

AMAN. Break off the eba and then swirl it around in the sauce.

And then grip it when you put it in your mouth.

AIDAN. This makes chopsticks look easy.

AMAN. How is it?

AIDAN. Yeah, decent.

>(**AIDAN** *is choking and dying of the spice.*)

AMAN. You can't handle the pepper, oh!

AIDAN. What'd you put in there?

AMAN. Scotch bonnets, make em hot!

AIDAN. You trying to kill me?

AMAN. Not at all, just show you about my culture…

    (**AIDAN** *is sitting back and relaxing.*)

AIDAN. Thank you. This is kind of freeing… relaxing…

AMAN. You never take time to relax, take a break, a holiday?

AIDAN. I have been nowhere other than Ireland.

AMAN. You haven't left the country?

AIDAN. No.

AMAN. But you've got a British passport. You can go anywhere in the world.

The pyramids in Egypt.

New York.

Tokyo.

AIDAN. Not everyone can afford to go to those places.

    (*Beat.*)

Is that what you want, a British passport?

AMAN. You don't understand, when I see a country it's through struggle, not a holiday.

You don't even use the things you have.

AIDAN. You don't know about my life.

AMAN. I know you have a business.

A home.

A family.

Can do anything you want…

Be happy.

AIDAN. Just be happy, as if it's that easy.

AMAN. Yes!

Your mum's death, you're not over that.

I can see it, feel it.

Seen many people die.

(*Silence.*)

But are you happy right now? This very second.

AIDAN. Yeah I think so but tomorrow –

AMAN. Now is all that matters.

AIDAN. So I should just stop doing what I'm doing.

My routine.

Therapist.

Everything I'm used to.

AMAN. Yeah, but if it's not making you happy?

(**AMAN** *stands up and starts taking off his top.*)

AIDAN. What are you doing?

AMAN. What makes me happy.

(**AMAN** *is down to his boxers, he encourages* **AIDAN** *to do the same.* **AIDAN** *strips off.* **AMAN** *runs offstage towards the water and we hear a splash.*)

AIDAN. You're mad.

AMAN. (*Offstage.*) Come on!

AIDAN. Coming.

(**AIDAN** *is getting changed and can feel his pills in his pocket. He looks at them before throwing them into the bushes. He runs offstage and we hear a splash as he lands in the water.*)

Scene Sixteen

(**LINTON** *walks on stage, suited and booted, with* **BILL** *trailing behind him.* **BILL**'s *got a camera to take pics of* **LINTON** *who has a high-vis vest on over his suit.*)

LINTON. Nothing but wasteland was here.

BILL. Impressive.

LINTON. The boys worked day and night to clear this space.

At first, they didn't like it and didn't want to get their hands dirty but once they got going. There was no stopping 'em.

BILL. And it's gonna be a skate park?

LINTON. I wasn't too keen on it but you've gotta give em something they are motivated by.

See that there.

(**LINTON** *is pointing out into the audience.*)

We're gonna sand down that wood and give it a nice finish.

(*Silence.*)

BILL. You should be proud of yourself mate.

LINTON. You'd think so.

But it's like no one barely notices.

They build that gallery and they've got all sorts turning out.

But when I do this, no one bats an eye.

BILL. Horses for courses.

LINTON. I just want it to mean something.

For our spaces to mean something.

To be used...

BILL. The kids like it, that's what counts.

LINTON. This was supposed to help boost my campaign... not so much as a whimper.

BILL. Those that know... know and that's all that counts...

LINTON. Doesn't turn it into votes though does it...

(*Silence.*)

That's why I'm counting on you.

BILL. Hey, I gave you a donation.

LINTON. I need people knocking on doors and getting the vote out.

BILL. Works keeping me busy.

LINTON. Really...

(**LINTON** *slams the newspaper into* **BILL**'*s chest.*)

'Running on empty, the refugee who found a home in Kent.'

BILL. They'll print what they want.

(**LINTON** *takes the paper off* **BILL** *and reads the article.*)

LINTON. "It's too early to say whether Hassan's running can improve to the top flight, but he's making strong progress. I can see him shining at the 10k distance and in cross country."

Local businessman – Bill Bradley.

BILL. I had to say something, he was asking for a quote.

The lad is talented.

You want me to just ignore his talent?

He can run 10k in under thirty minutes.

At twenty one.

LINTON. You talk about him like you know him? That was supposed to be my headline and you robbed it from me.

BILL. I don't decide what they print. I'm just helping the kid out. It's the right thing to do.

They're not as bad as you think. Polite, quiet, clean – keep to themselves.

LINTON. And that's enough for you?

BILL. I'm just saying when you get speaking to them, you see they're just trying to get a better life. No different to Lin coming from Thailand.

LINTON. My wife came here legally!

BILL. I didn't mean anything by it.

LINTON. You know he's taking illegal jobs down by the DIY shop, I've seen him with the rest of them.

BILL. No. No. He said he wasn't.

I had a word and he said...

LINTON. And you believe him?

BILL. Listen, you're angry.

I know you put a lot of effort into this place but no need to put the boot in.

LINTON. What?

BILL. Ever since you started hanging around those kooks in the loony party.

You've been getting stranger.

Plain weird.

I've seen you on social media.

Posting those weird videos – like some sort of conspiracy theorist.

You're changing mate.

LINTON. I'm changing? You're the one that doesn't even know what's going on under your own roof.

BILL. What'd you mean?

LINTON. Oh God, you have got the foggiest... Aidan knew the refugee boys before they came to the hotel. He had you thinking they just showed up on your doorstep when he really sent them there.

BILL. Nah... he would've said. And why are you getting onto me anyway, having a go. I'm here you aren't I?

LINTON. I'm just saying it how it is. The community ain't happy about it mate.

BILL. Community, I am the community, been here my whole life

LINTON. You got a business to run but this ain't the way.

(Pause.)

Selling out.

BILL. Selling out! Is that what you think I'm doing? Or is it the politician speaking?

LINTON. I tell you things aren't good, people aren't happy but you don't want to hear it.

But I said it now.

And now it's on you.

BILL. What is...?

(Silence.)

LINTON. At some stage, we've all gotta make choices...or pay for them.

I've got my hustings later this week and I want you to take a stand with me.

BILL. I told you, that party, those people ain't for me... me and you, we're good but that... them...

LINTON. It's a chance to show whose side you're on and I expect you to be there.

(**LINTON** *barges offstage, past* **BILL**.)

Scene Seventeen

*(**AIDAN** and **AMAN** are in the kitchen of the
Dalby Hotel. **AIDAN** is engrossed in his phone
looking at samples of different paint colours
while **AMAN** is cleaning.)*

AIDAN. Everything's so old in this place.

AMAN. So why don't you change it?

AIDAN. Can't afford it.

AMAN. Gotta spend money to make money...

(Beat.)

If you had all the money you needed, what would you
do to this place?

*(**AIDAN** is walking around the room thinking
about his vision.)*

AIDAN. I'd take through this wall – make it an open plan
area.

Have a counter – so customers could put in their orders
for food.

I'd get a double oven, electric cooker...

AMAN. A dishwasher?

AIDAN. That's why I've got you.

*(**AMAN** throws the kitchen towel at **AIDAN** in
jest.)*

Maybe some new tiles.

AMAN. Do it.

*(**AIDAN** is looking on his phone for ideas for
inspiration.)*

AIDAN. I saw this before.

AMAN. I like the blue...

AIDAN. If we're going to convince Dad to invest, we best do a good job here. You missed a spot.

AMAN. Where?

> (While **AMAN** is looking confused, **AIDAN** dips his fingers into the bucket of soapy water and flicks it at **AMAN**.)

Oi.

> (**AMAN** grabs the bucket of water and moves towards **AIDAN**.)

AIDAN. You wouldn't...

Aman!

> (**AMAN** flicks some of the water on **AIDAN**, they are spraying each other with water and are in hysterics, before they come together in an embrace.)

HASSAN. Aman...

> (They back off one another when they see **HASSAN** approach them.)

AMAN. Hassan.

> (**AMAN** pushes **AIDAN** off of him.)

You alright bro...

> (Silence.)

AIDAN. I'm gonna get rid of this dirty water.

AMAN. Do you want me to help?

AIDAN. No it's alright.

*(**AIDAN** leaves. **AMAN** is making his way around the room attempting to clean up the mess.)*

AMAN. You been training again?

HASSAN. Yeah.

AMAN. Getting good... running faster.

I saw you in the paper.

(Beat.)

HASSAN. But you never came to the race.

AMAN. I would've...

HASSAN. I thought you were supposed to be helping him, not making a mess?

*(**HASSAN** is pointing to all the water on the floor.)*

Wetin you dey do here Aman?

AMAN. Nutting...

I'm working.

Working like you said.

*(**HASSAN** takes a seat exhausted.)*

HASSAN. I need you to step up, no more games... You didn't come here to be with that boy.

You don't think I see you two.

AMAN. You see it but don't want to talk about it.

I haven't got anyone else to talk to about my feelings other than a brother who –

HASSAN. You're going to mess things up.

AMAN. Why?

HASSAN. You can't see. This is where we live, our lives.

What happens if you two have an argument? He kicks us out?

You don't tink.

(**AMAN** *walks up to* **HASSAN***'s face.*)

AMAN. I'm not a little boy.

HASSAN. Ode.

AMAN. Don't call me that!

(*Silence.*)

HASSAN. And Bill?

Huh?

Does he know?

(*Beat.*)

AMAN. Of course not.

Aidan's not...

It's not good for us.

HASSAN. Who's us?

You and him?

Or me and you?

Which one is it?

AMAN. It's not you or him.

Why does it have to be that way?

You're my brother but you need to stop trying to control me.

(*Silence.*)

HASSAN. OK.

> (**HASSAN** *backs away with his hands up in acceptance of* **AMAN***'s stance.*)

I don't need this wahala oh.

You do it your way.

But don't expect me to come to rescue you, Aman.

> (**HASSAN** *walks out on* **AMAN.***)*

Scene Eighteen

*(**AIDAN** and **AMAN** are sitting across the table from one another in a coffee shop. **AMAN** is spaced out just staring at the cup of coffee.)*

AIDAN. You gonna drink it?

*(**AMAN** takes a sip of the drink.)*

AMAN. You know coffee grows in Africa... in de East...

They call it black gold.

A way out of poverty.

Farmers break their backs to grow the coffee bean.

Then I come to Europe.

See people, sitting and chatting.

Sipping.

Especially in Italy.

Oh they love coffee.

AIDAN. Italy?

AMAN. Yes when we travel through Libya to Italy.

My journey takes me through the Sahara to Italy.

Then across Europe to France.

I see everyone loves this.

But they hate us.

*(**AMAN** holds up the cup of coffee.)*

But it shows we are all connected.

Related.

No matter what they say.

AIDAN. I've never thought of it like that.

AMAN. Because you've never had to.

Here you just go up to the man.

Make your order.

Latte.

Soya Milk.

Decaf.

Extra hot.

A little bit of cinnamon.

The spices.

The coffee.

All of it comes from somewhere. No?

But to you, it's just a drink.

AIDAN. OK...

AMAN. What I'm saying is, you and me – we can look at the same thing and see something different...

(Silence.)

AIDAN. Why'd you go quiet on me before we were... you're not...?

AMAN. No.

AIDAN. You said nothing after Hassan walked in on us like that.

AMAN. I don't enjoy lying to my brother.

AIDAN. You're not scared of him are you?

AMAN. Hassan... no...

AIDAN. Cos you can say if he's... he can't stop you from being out here. There are laws that protect us.

(*Beat.*)

What?

AMAN. It's funny you think I'm afraid of my brother, when
you shake as soon as your dad walks into the room.

(*Beat.*)

Does your dad know about your art? The things you
want to do?

AIDAN. A letter came recently from an art college I'd been
looking at.

(**AIDAN** *takes the letter out of his pocket.*)

But he just dismissed it and didn't really want to talk
about it with me... so I just tried to bury it but I can't
stop thinking and dreaming about it...

AMAN. And what would you do there?

AIDAN. Study art and graphic design.

AMAN. Then that is what you should do.

AIDAN. As if it is as easy as that.

AMAN. Why not? You have to tell him what you want
Aidan...

AIDAN. It's OK, I'll tell him when I'm ready...

I just need your patience... support...

AMAN. You don't need me! You are so talented, if I had
half the talent you do...

You just need to take steps.

Small steps.

AIDAN. Things that are normal for other people scare me.

Things in your head that look easy they're not for me.

It's hard.

Bloody hard.

I think I can't do it but I just freeze.

And then it's like I'm stuck.

And I can't get out.

AMAN. Where is this college?

AIDAN. London.

AMAN. Say word. Aidan I've been wanting to get out of here, get to London. It's a city that is me, where I'd fit in.

> (**AMAN** *stands up full of excitement.*)

We could go clubbing when wanted, get a flat of our own, eat in the best restaurants...

I can't spend anymore of my life or my time, just hanging around here. It's driving me crazy. I need to get out of this place.

AIDAN. You'll get in trouble with the Home Office.

AMAN. Like they care what I do.

AIDAN. We can't just up and leave.

AMAN. Why not?

AIDAN. My Dad.

What about Hassan?

> (*Silence.*)

AMAN. Like you said he doesn't understand... I need this.

You need this.

For yourself.

Your art.

Or you never will.

This is your chance. Our chance.

(**AMAN** *holds* **AIDAN**'s *hand and looks at him.*)

Scene Nineteen

(BILL is sitting to the side as LINTON has a lectern and mic in front of him. We can hear the background noise and grumble of the audience. LINTON rises to address them.)

LINTON. Good evening.

If you could keep quiet at the back, we've got several items to get through.

(The background noise of the audience dampens down.)

Thank you.

(LINTON shuffles his papers and clears his throat.)

Now we know how important this time is for our local democracy. The election is weeks away and the Tories are making you believe they're the party to clean things up. But they don't believe local politics matter. But right here is where actual change happens!

(Pause.)

So I will not sugarcoat it, censor it or cover it up, because there are things that need to be said... For too long we have sat back while the very face of our community has changed. Where a foreign couple moves in down the road to you.

(LINTON leans into the mic.)

It starts as one or two.

Then within twenty-four hours.

You get the grandparents.

The in-laws and their kids are moving in.

What started out as a family of four, quickly becomes ten to fifteen.

One house on the street is occupied.

And then three or four more.

Before you know it, the face of the whole street has changed.

Filled with rubbish.

Needles.

Your kids can't play outside anymore.

And you no longer recognise where you're living.

>   (**LINTON** *turns over the page of his speech.*)

Now some of them are lovely people.

Lovely families.

But fifteen living in one house?

The costs to the state?

When you have put nothing into the system.

You shouldn't be allowed to take anything out of it.

Simple as.

It's not fair.

It is not right.

It's not just.

But this is modern-day Britain.

And you can tell me I'm fear-mongering, creating divisions.

>   (**BILL** *is moving about uncomfortable with*
>   **LINTON** *drawing attention to him.*)

The middle classes tell us to believe in regeneration.

The Turner Gallery.

Hipster cafes.

Immigration will save our town.

I say, you sir are killing our town.

Killing our families

Killing our communities.

And if you don't believe so just ask Bill.

Bill stand up.

(**BILL** *rises to his feet.*)

He has a business that's been standing in this community for over thirty years.

And all he has done is try to help.

Be a part of the solution.

Hell, he's even taken them in.

BILL. Linton…

LINTON. Don't be shy.

It's a good thing.

A noble thing to do.

But the project isn't working is it?

BILL. Well we've had our difficulties but…

LINTON. The lad, the runner he's working illegally and I'm sure the other one's no good.

BILL. They're young…

LINTON. But are they? What do you know about them?

BILL. I've…

LINTON. You only know what they lie to you about.

BILL. What are you doing?

LINTON. Look at how they've tricked Bill into spending his time, money and effort to help them - leaving him out of pocket.

How many people in Margate have been rehoused recently?

BILL. I don't know.

LINTON. Been given the opportunity these lads have?

(Silence.)

You see how brainwashed we've become!

*(**BILL** departs the stage, embarrassed by **LINTON**.)*

You've got a choice in this election.

One that takes you down the path of becoming forgotten about.

Or one in which we take control of our futures.

I know which one I'll be choosing.

*(We hear the applause from the audience, **LINTON** basking in his own glory.)*

Scene Twenty

> *(Situated in the kitchen of Bradley's apartment in the hotel, **AMAN** is sitting opposite **BILL** at the table – **AIDAN** is laying out the food.)*

AIDAN. Could you pass me the veg?

It's on the kitchen counter.

BILL. I told you I'm not eating kale anymore. Gives me the runs.

AIDAN. It's rocket.

BILL. Same thing.

> *(**HASSAN** enters the room flustered and dumps his bag on the floor.)*

AIDAN. Thanks for coming.

BILL. You done your evening training?

HASSAN. Not yet.

AIDAN. Give him a break.

BILL. If you want to be the best…

AIDAN. At least let him eat first.

BILL. I'm just saying when it comes to the greats there are no days off.

HASSAN. I'll go for a run tonight.

BILL. Five blocks of ten. Good lad.

> *(Beat.)*

HASSAN. I need to wash my hands.

> *(While **AIDAN** is still sorting out the food and table placements, **HASSAN** leaves to go and wash his hands.)*

AIDAN. I'd thought we'd check out one of the Folk Week events after dinner.

AMAN. Folk Week?

AIDAN. It's like a music and dance festival which happens every year.

AMAN. Yeah.

BILL. I don't think that's your thing.

More for kids/older members of the community.

AIDAN. Some stuff for young people too.

BILL. Yeah but people might not want them –

AIDAN. Dad!

> *(Silence.)*

> *(**HASSAN** comes back on stage.)*

BILL. So what have we got here then?

AIDAN. Roast, some veg, gravy.

BILL. You trying to fatten me up?

AIDAN. Don't think that's possible.

> *(**AMAN** leans over to carve up the chicken when he notices all eyes on him. **AMAN** sits back down and **BILL** stands up to take the knife and fork off him.)*

It's Dad's thing...

BILL. It's not a thing, there's a special technique to it.

You've gotta get the balance right, between cutting enough meat and skin.

HASSAN. Is it halal?

BILL. Halal…

HASSAN. The meat?

AIDAN. Yes, I went to the Halal butchers in town.

HASSAN. Good.

> (**BILL** *sits back down in his seat and puts the carving knife back on the table, his job incomplete.*)

AIDAN. You haven't finished…

BILL. It's ruined.

AIDAN. What?

BILL. I can't eat that.

AIDAN. Dad it's just chicken.

BILL. What's really going on here?

AIDAN. What'd you mean?

BILL. We're playing happy families… It's weird…

AIDAN. It's just a meal.

BILL. It doesn't fit.

> (**BILL** *points at the chicken.*)

AIDAN. It tastes the same… It's just different…

BILL. If that's the case why can't they just eat our chicken?

AIDAN. I can't believe we're talking about chickens.

BILL. When in Rome… It'll help you fit in.

AMAN. Fit in?

BILL. We all have to change a bit.

AMAN. You can do all of that stuff and still…

BILL. No more excuses. Please.

AMAN. What I can't change is the colour of my skin!

BILL. Oh here we go...

AMAN. Or my name.

BILL. If you put the effort in, you'll be fine.

AMAN. If you can't see it, you won't get it...

AIDAN. That's what this is about. Getting to know each other...

AMAN. I'm not a puppet, in your show.

BILL. No, you're just a rent-a-mouth.

AMAN. Suppose you want me to be a sell-out like my brother then instead?

How high can you jump?

How fast can you run?

You a slave Hassan?

HASSAN. Shut up your mout.

AMAN. No.

BILL. He's on his soapbox now!

AMAN. You think you know everyting...

BILL. I know a dosser when I see one...

AIDAN. He ain't lazy Dad.

AMAN. Don't let him do this... tell him Aidan...

BILL. What... You two keeping secrets now?

AIDAN. No!

AMAN. Tell him what you want...

AIDAN. I don't want to talk about this.

BILL. Can you stop trying to fill his head with nonsense?

AIDAN. Can we just eat?

AMAN. Aidan...

AIDAN. What!

> *(Beat.)*

AMAN. I thought we'd agree. That this was our time and you're not saying anything?

Won't acknowledge me in front of your Dad.

AIDAN. Why'd you think I called this meal?

AMAN. But you're too scared to say anything?

> *(Silence.)*

(To **BILL**.*)* Your son has been getting with the refugee.

BILL. Aidan?

AIDAN. Dad it's a –

BILL. A fling, a dalliance, a flirt, it means nothing.

AMAN. Meaning nothing? We're going away to London together...

HASSAN. You're going to leave and not tell me...?

AMAN. Bro... I ...

BILL. He's having us on.

AMAN. Why is this all a joke to you?

> *(**BILL** goes up to **AIDAN** and is pleading with his son.)*

BILL. Cos... cos... me and you... we're good. Building the business back together, you wouldn't let him come between us.

AIDAN. I've been meaning to...

BILL. Nah, nah, nah. Hold that thought.

> (**BILL** *goes offstage to go and retrieve a letter.*)

AMAN. Aidan, say something. Now's your –

> (**BILL** *reappears back onstage.*)

BILL. The business... the business.... I was thinking about handing it over to you even got the registration papers here.

> (**BILL** *holds up a document.*)

BILL. Aidan... putting it in your name... cos you've stepped up the last few months and I want you to have this legacy.

AMAN. So you're trying to buy him.

> (**AIDAN** *is stuck in the middle of the men and isn't sure what to say.*)

HASSAN. Aman, maybe we should go.

AMAN. *(To* **BILL***.)* Why are you so scared of him leaving, living out his dreams, doing his own thing?

HASSAN. Aman... where is all of this coming from?

AMAN. Bro I –

BILL. See his own brother doesn't even have a clue. How can you trust a guy like that Aidan?

AMAN. Shut up.

> *(Silence.)*

BILL. You know what, it's time you and your brother move on, best for all of us.

> (**AMAN** *turns toward* **AIDAN** *sitting at the table.*)

AMAN. Aidan. I'm begging you. If there was ever a time for you to do what you want, it's now.

> (**AIDAN** *is numb, silent and not moving.*)

Just say the word and we go.

HASSAN. Leave it bro, he never saw it like you did.

> (**HASSAN** *is consoling* **AMAN** *and taking him away from the room.*)

BILL. And don't think I don't know about you either, going behind my back and working.

> (**AIDAN** *is ashamed and doesn't know where to look.* **BILL** *points over to* **HASSAN**'*s bag.*)

After I stuck my neck out for you, you betrayed me like that.

I'm gonna have to report it.

You'll be sanctioned. Lose your immigration status.

AIDAN. What are you doing?

BILL. I knew this was a bad idea from the start.

AIDAN. You want to drive everyone out of my life.

> (*Beat.*)

Cos if you do, it'll only be you, here – alone.

BILL. Have you heard what's going on out there? People aren't happy and it's being directed at us.

AIDAN. I'm just saying I'm tired… I can't be here anymore.

BILL. But I'm handing it all over to you.

AIDAN. So I should be grateful for this fucking place!

These fucking walls! Not anymore

(**AIDAN** *goes to leave with* **HASSAN** *and* **AMAN**.)

BILL. You don't walk out on me… I raised you.

(**BILL** *is frothing at the mouth and picks up the carving knife on the table and points at* **AMAN** *accusingly.*)

You think you can just take my son away from me and ruin my life.

(**AMAN** *walks up to* **BILL**, *ballsy but not scared of the knife in his hand and whispers in his ear.*)

AMAN. I just did and there is nothing you can do about it.

(**AMAN** *turns his back on* **BILL**, *who goes for him with the knife,* **HASSAN** *comes to shield his brother. Who falls to the floor.*)

BILL. No, no, no. Not you. Hassan. Hassan.

(**AIDAN** *and* **AMAN** *look at* **HASSAN** *who collapses into the arms of* **BILL**. *A state of shock, a place none of them expected them to be.*)

Scene Twenty One

(**AMAN** *walks into the hotel garden where* **AIDAN** *is digging up some plants and watering them.* **AIDAN** *is so consumed with what he is doing he doesn't notice* **AMAN** *behind him.*)

AMAN. Aidan?

(**AIDAN** *looks over at* **AMAN***; he isn't sure how to address him so keeps on weeding the garden.*)

These weeds just keep on growing. I mean, I put the weed killer on them but it doesn't make any difference.

(**AIDAN** *is trying to yank the weed out but can't get any progress.*)

AIDAN. It just won't come out.

AMAN. Can you please leave the fucking weeds alone.

(*Silence.*)

(**AIDAN** *walks away from the plants, takes his gloves off and sits.*)

AIDAN. I'd been calling you but no answer... left messages but no answer.

This place, it's taking up all my time, the suppliers, cleaning, food –

AMAN. Feels like you're ignoring me.

AIDAN. No.

AMAN. Then look at me when I'm speaking to you.

AIDAN. I don't know how to deal with it... your brother... my Dad... I.... I'm struggling.

I'm sorry.

Sorry for bringing you all here.

Sorry for what happened... I... I....don't know what to say....

> (**AIDAN** *is panicking and* **AMAN** *has to hug him to calm him down.*)

AMAN. Breathe, just breathe.

AIDAN. Why did you come back?

AMAN. I don't know.

> *(Beat.)*

I try to block it out of my mind.

Erase it but the memories keep playing.

Our memories.

But my mama, she always says face forwards not backwards.

So that's what I'm trying to do.

But I had to see your face. I didn't want that... to be the last memory I had of you.

> (**AIDAN** *looks down at* **AMAN**'s *bags on the floor.*)

AIDAN. Where have you been staying?

AMAN. A hostel.

AIDAN. I'm sorry I can't have you at the hotel.

It's not really the best place for you right now...

AMAN. No.

AIDAN. Where will you go?

AMAN. London.

AIDAN. London?

AMAN. Yes. Like we talked about.

AIDAN. So much has happened, I've been trying to sort out things with my dad and this place.

I hadn't thought...

AMAN. I'm catching the train this evening... and I don't know if I'm mad for saying this but... we had a plan and I'm going to stick to it. .

> (**AMAN** *goes and picks up the plant they planted together.*)

We can either choose to die or live....

> (**HASSAN** *gently offers the plant to* **AIDAN** *before leaving.*)

Scene Twenty Two

(**AMAN**'s at a train station, when he gets a call on the tannoy for the train to London leaving in five minutes. He's checking the time on his watch and moving about on the stage anxiously looking for who might appear to the side of the stage. He doesn't think anybody is coming and is walking offstage in disappointment, when we are shocked to see him bump into **HASSAN**.)

HASSAN. It's usually you who is late, not me.

AMAN. Bro...

(**AMAN** hugs his brother.)

HASSAN. Easy now.

AMAN. Sorry.

HASSAN. Ah Aman, why are you crying now?

AMAN. I don't know. Everyting that go bring us here. But we are together. Brudda's.

(**AMAN** and **HASSAN** do their special handshake before **HASSAN** lets go.)

Wetin go happen?

HASSAN. You go change. I go change.

AMAN. But it go make us stronger, eh?

HASSAN. This place is no go be for me.

AMAN. You'll like London much better than this place, let's go.

HASSAN. It's not home. You wanted this Aman. I came because I was scared of what might happen to you, and thought I could help de family. But I'm running out of lives, how many tings nearly happened over the last two years?

AMAN. He should go to prison.

HASSAN. I no go press charges.

AMAN. But he nearly murdered you!

HASSAN. And how many other people have done bad things to me before on this journey...I just want to be with my family.

AMAN. What are you saying?

HASSAN. I go find a way to fly back to Naija.

AMAN. Are you stupid?

HASSAN. It is better for me. Better for my family.

AMAN. And me. Am I not your family? I won't be able to see you again if you go back.

HASSAN. You don't need me anymore. I am your brother, not your keeper.

> (**AMAN** *is getting emotional holding onto his big brother. They are both crying.*)

Be sensible. You go call me when you get to London.

> (*The brothers watch each other from across the stage for the last time wondering when the next time maybe they see each other.* **AMAN** *is sitting on a bench devastated, feeling like he lost everything.* **HASSAN** *is watching on from afar, and is met by* **AIDAN** *on the side of the stage.*)

(*To* **AIDAN.**) Take care of him.

> (**AIDAN** *nods in acknowledgement of the request.* **AMAN,** *who has his head in his*

hands crying, is unaware of **AIDAN**'s *presence as he comes and takes a seat next to him.)*

AIDAN. The guy said last minute tickets are double the price, but I thought it was worth it.

AMAN. Aidan.

(**AIDAN** *takes* **AMAN**'s *hand and sits.)*

AIDAN. You were right. We face forwards, not backwards.

(**AIDAN** *and* **AMAN** *are sitting on the bench looking out into the audience and contemplating in hope of what their future might hold.)*

END

Ingram Content Group UK Ltd.
Milton Keynes UK
UKHW021332130623
423374UK00026B/204

9 780573 133800